FAITH WORKS

ANDRÉ GORHAM

FAITH WORKS

Copyright © 2005 by André Gorham

ISBN: 0-9770398-0-3

Published by

LIFEBRIDGE
BOOKS
P.O. BOX 49428
CHARLOTTE, NC 28277

Printed in the United States of America.

DEDICATION

*This book is dedicated to the memory
of my grandmother, Eliza Beamon Williams,
who took me to Sunday School where I learned
about the faith of David, Daniel and Joseph; my
good friend Bobby Ray Clements, who encouraged
me to follow my dreams; my wife, Cynthia, and my
three boys, André II, Caleb and Daniel, who are
a fulfillment of a promise from God to me.*

CONTENTS

INTRODUCTION

Faith is one of the most misunderstood concepts in our society. For many, it is simply a word used when talking about being optimistic or having confidence.

To me, however, faith is much more than a concept. It is a way of life based on biblical principles which affect everything I do. As you will see, the reason I know faith *works* is because of personal experience. It has brought hope and healing and spiritual growth to our family.

On these pages you will learn the difference between faith and believing—and how to remove the obstacles to receiving form God. Plus, we will answer many questions, including, "Where does faith come from?" and "How do I receive it?"

I want you to understand that even though faith is a spiritual force, it will always be manifest in the natural—a tangible, visible, physical reality.

Let me encourage you to read this book with an open Bible. When you see a scripture reference, turn to God's Word, read the verses in context and apply them to your life.

It is my prayer this book will expand your understanding of faith, hope, expectation and belief. Most important, I want you to discover how to use these divine gifts in your personal life to claim God's best.

– André Gorham

CHAPTER 1

THE "IF" OF FAITH

In our pragmatic world focused on logic and science, millions quickly dismiss the concept of faith. As one man told me, "I only believe what I see with my eyes and feel with my hands."

Yet, if we would stop for a moment, we would recognize our daily reliance on belief and trust. We have faith the sun will rise tomorrow morning—or that an oncoming car won't swerve into our path. When we take a child to be vaccinated, we have total faith in both the doctor and the medicine.

If people can place such unwavering trust in man-made, physical objects, why is it so difficult for them to have faith in the Creator who set the world into motion?

I am delighted you have chosen to take this spiritual journey with me. Why? Because you will discover that faith in God is not a nebulous concept or an abstract idea. It is a God-given principle of living that—when activated—will release the floodgates of heaven's blessing.

Here are just a few of the questions we will be answering:

- What is the difference between faith and believing?
- Who is entitled to have faith in God?
- How do you know when you are "in faith"?
- What is the "trying" of your faith?
- How is faith received?
- What is the "prayer of faith"?

IT IS CONDITIONAL

From the title of this book you already know I believe faith *works*, yet God has placed stipulations on *how* we are to receive from Him. You see, we have been created as free moral agents with the power to choose between good and evil, right and wrong. In fact, His blessings are always conditional on our obedience.

> HIS BLESSINGS ARE ALWAYS CONDITIONAL ON OUR OBEDIENCE.

One of the shortest, yet most powerful words in scripture contains just two letters; the word is "if."

The Almighty told the children of Israel, *"And it shall come to pass, if thou shalt hearken diligently unto the voice of the Lord thy God, to observe and to do all his commandments which*

10

I command thee this day, that the Lord thy God will set thee on high above all nations of the earth: And all these blessings shall come on thee, and overtake thee, if thou shalt hearken unto the voice of the Lord thy God" (Deuteronomy 28:1-2).

Simply stated: *"If* you will obey, I will bless."

NOT QUANTITY, BUT QUALITY

Centuries later, when God sent His Son, Jesus, to be born as Man and teach the divine message of the Father, we find the same "if."

The disciples came to Him with this request: *"Lord, increase our faith"* (Luke 17:5).

It is obvious, that after spending time with Jesus and personally observing the tremendous miracles He achieved as a result of His faith, they wanted to tap into this same access with the Father.

Even though Jesus had previously told them the significance of faith in seeing prayer answered, they still did not fully understand. This is evident since they addressed the subject in regards to quantity—assuming the reason they were not having the dynamic results the Lord consistently achieved was because they didn't have *enough* of this substance called "faith."

The same problem affects believers today.

Despite this, Jesus immediately responds to His disciples by telling them it is not the *quantity* of their

11

faith, rather the *quality* which makes the difference.

Jesus replied, *"If ye had faith as a grain of mustard seed, ye might say unto this sycamine tree, Be thou plucked up by the root, and be thou planted in the sea; and it should obey you"* (Luke 17:6).

HOW MUCH?

Since a mustard seed is one of the smallest seeds in existence, it is clear that *amount* is not the issue when it comes to faith.

> EITHER YOU BELIEVE IN GOD OR YOU PLACE YOUR TRUST IN SOME OTHER PERSON OR THING.

In a certain sense our personal faith resembles money—neither good nor bad. It could even be classified as neutral. Once money comes into the possession of people, the determination of how positive or negative it is becomes evident. Obviously in the hands of a drug dealer its use would be substantially different than in the hands of a missionary. However, the money itself has no moral character.

Essentially faith is similar—neither big nor small—just simply faith. Either you believe in God or you place your trust in some other person or thing. This is why Jesus tells us to, *"Have faith in God"* (Mark 11:22).

REMOVING OBSTACLES

Neither the Father, Son or the Holy Spirit ever assumes you have faith. Jesus does not say to His disciples, *"Since* ye had faith," but *"If* ye had faith."

It is important to understand that "if" could be the determining factor between receiving *something* from the Lord or receiving *nothing.*

This same powerful two-letter word is repeated by Jesus as He says, *"If ye have faith, and doubt not, ye shall not only do this which is done to the fig tree, but also if ye shall say unto this mountain, Be thou removed, and be thou cast into the sea; it shall be done* (Matthew 21:21).

In both examples, the Master declares, "if we had faith we would speak" and the obstacle would be removed—whether it be a tree (Luke 17:6) or a mountain (Matthew 21:21).

THE DISCIPLES FAILED

Some have read the above words and have spoken to situations with presumption rather than faith. This won't work!

Once, a man who was in a crowd approached Jesus and knelt before Him, pleading, *"Lord, have mercy on my son: for he is a lunatic, and sore vexed: for ofttimes he falleth into the fire, and oft into the water. And I brought him to thy disciples, and they could not cure him"* (Matthew 17:15-16).

The disciples tried to imitate the works of Jesus, but they failed. He turned and rebuked them with these words: *"O faithless and perverse generation, how long shall I be with you? How long shall I suffer you?"* (v.17).

After asking for the boy to be brought to Him, Jesus *"rebuked the devil; and he departed out of him: and the child was cured from that very hour"* (v.18).

Apparently, the disciples prayed for the boy, yet without faith in their hearts. If you have faith you will speak not *about* nor *around*, rather *to* those things to which you are exercising your belief.

THE SOURCE OF FAITH

It is only natural to ask, "How do we acquire mountain-moving faith? What is the source?"

According to scripture, *"...faith cometh by hearing, and hearing by the word of God"* (Romans 10:17). It is only when we hear the *Word* true faith comes alive.

Let me show you how this will impact your life—and the lives of those you love.

Once faith arrives you will no longer need to ask "What should I do?" The Bible declares, *"...the prayer of faith shall save the sick, and the Lord shall raise him up* (James 5:15).

What is this "prayer of faith"? It is the result of having the Word so hidden in your heart, absolutely nothing can dislodge or shake it. As James tells us, *"If any of you lack wisdom, let him ask of God, that giveth to all men liberally, and upbraideth not; and it shall be given him. But let him ask in faith, nothing wavering. For he that wavereth is like a wave of the sea driven with the wind and tossed"* (James 1:5-6).

Since faith is based on hearing, you need to ask yourself, "What have I been listening to? Have I been hearing the Word of God?"

Next, what you hear, you will speak!

> **WHEN FAITH IS DELIVERED FROM THE ONLY SOURCE, THE SPEAKING WILL TAKE CARE OF ITSELF.**

Of course, we must, study, feed and meditate on scripture, but most important is our willingness to *hear* the Word of God. Then, when faith is delivered from the only true source, the speaking will take care of itself.

BOTH HEARD AND SEEN

The two areas where faith is evidenced in a believer's life are (1) what he *says* with his mouth and (2) what he *does*.

These must be totally based on the Word of God. If you have faith, then the reference point for what you say and do will always be what you believe from scripture. As a result faith will be both heard (which comes from what you say) and seen (which comes from what you do). This is how you will know you are "in faith."

Just as sunlight follows the rising of the sun, actions always follow belief—and it begins to be evidenced in your words and behavior. For example, you "do the Word" when you say what the Bible says concerning your life instead of talking about circumstances.

> JUST AS SUNLIGHT FOLLOWS THE RISING OF THE SUN, ACTIONS ALWAYS FOLLOW BELIEF.

Another demonstration of "faith works" is to do the opposite of what you fear. For example, you may be afraid to give according to the scripture which declares, *"Give, and it shall be given unto you; good measure, pressed down, and shaken together, and running over"* (Luke 6:38).

Even if you think this will not work, obey the Lord anyway. Give according to the degree you are able to believe. Start with fifty cents and develop greater faith from there.

THE EVIDENCE

When what is planted on the inside begins to grow and bloom, you will see the *evidence.*

If you have faith, you will have corresponding actions to what you say you believe. Again, faith should not only be *heard*, but also *seen*.

James the disciple (and half-brother of Jesus) vividly describes the faith-works relationship. Apparently, people in his day erroneously assumed a great deal about this issue.

He begins by asking, *"What doth it profit, my brethren, though a man say he hath faith, and have not works? Can faith save him?"* (James 2:14).

James uses the example of a person finding a brother or sister without clothing or food, saying to them, "Go. I wish you well. Stay warm and well fed."

He asks, "If you don't take care of the physical needs, what good is it?" Then James adds, *"Even so faith, if it hath not works, is dead"* (v.17). In this sense, dead means barren or unable to produce fruit or results.

Next, there is a powerful statement which qualifies and even summarizes James' intent when dealing with what people *say* they have concerning faith and what they *really* possess. He declares: *"Yea, a man may say, Thou hast faith, and I have works: show me thy faith without thy works* [he infers here that it cannot be done], *and I will show thee my faith by my works"* (v.18).

What a strong message! In other words, you will know there is faith by the actions which accompany and correspond to my belief.

DEAD OR ALIVE?

Today, we can ask, "How do you know I have faith unless you—God, angels, humans and demons—can see it? Faith, though it is a spiritual force, will always be manifest in the natural.

James continues by asking a question with an obvious answer: *"But wilt thou know, O vain man, that faith without works is dead?"* (v.20).

He points out how Abraham was justified by works when he offered his son, Isaac, upon the altar, then poignantly explains, *"Seest thou how faith wrought with his works, and by works was faith made perfect?"* (v.22).

James is telling us faith operated in *conjunction* and *harmony* with his works to produce certain desired results. He adds, *"And the scripture was fulfilled which saith, Abraham believed God, and it was imputed unto him for righteousness: and he was called the Friend of God"* (v.23).

Works which correspond with what you believe fulfills scripture. We are all friends of Jehovah when we do what we say we believe concerning the Word of God.

IT TAKES THE SPIRIT

The passage concludes with, *"For as the body without the spirit is dead, so faith without works is dead also"* (v.26).

This is an eternal truth. Minus the spirit, the body will never produce anything. No blood will flow, no carbon dioxide exchange will occur, no ideas will be expressed. There will be no fruit of any kind from a dead body. Nothing!

In summary, there is no such thing as Bible faith without action. To put it another way: *your "faith works" are the consummation of what you believe.*

ROOFTOP FAITH

Here is a marvelous example of how faith becomes visible.

In Capernaum, Jesus was preaching in a home, and four men carried a man who was sick of the palsy. However, because of the crowd, they could not bring him close to the Master.

So with action grounded in total faith, the men climbed up on the roof and began tearing through it—opening up a hole big enough for the paralyzed man and his mat to be lowered down below.

> **THERE IS NO SUCH THING AS BIBLE FAITH WITHOUT ACTION.**

The Bible records, *"When Jesus saw their faith, he said unto the sick of the palsy, Son, thy sins be forgiven thee"* (Mark 2:5).

Scripture does not say, "When He saw them let the person down," or "When He saw them uncover the roof." The Holy Spirit, through the writing of Mark, states emphatically, *"When Jesus saw their faith..."*

These four men *believed* if they could just get to Jesus, He would heal the man they were carrying. As a result, they were not deterred by the crowds or embarrassed by what people might think as they tore open the roof. Their *believing* removed all fears, concerns and doubts—and compelled them to come into the presence of the Lord Jesus Christ.

No doubt, many in the throng saw only their bold actions, yet Jesus saw their genuine faith. What a dynamic difference!

PLEASING GOD

Is faith in God reserved for only a select few? Absolutely not. It is for all! The Bible declares, *"It is written in the prophets, And they shall be all taught of God. Every man therefore that hath heard, and hath learned of the Father, cometh unto me"* (John 6:45).

Don't expect to be a man or woman of strong belief overnight. It takes time. As James writes, *"...the trying of your faith worketh patience. But let patience have her perfect work, that ye may be perfect and entire, wanting nothing"* (James 1:3-4).

The purpose of our faith is not to demonstrate what a marvelous saint of God we have become, or to call attention to our spiritual development. No. Our only objective is to please the Lord. As the Bible states, *"...without faith it is impossible to please him: for he that cometh to God must believe that he is, and that he is a rewarder of them that diligently seek him"* (Hebrews 11:6).

Faith is at the core of our spiritual life. It opens the door to salvation, healing and unlimited blessings. Most important it allows us to worship the Lord from the depths of our heart.

You will never need to question or worry "if" you have faith when you begin with the basics. Open your Bible and start to hear what God's Word is saying to you.

CHAPTER 2

THE POWER
OF BELIEVING

There is a place in God and in our dealings with His Word where our believing becomes as tangible and as three-dimensional as the physical existence around us.

In the world of faith and belief we constantly confront the impossible and insurmountable. However, we can stand back and watch natural circumstances and situations melt like wax under the heavy onslaught of faith in God's Word. This is true because we stand on the declaration of Jesus: *"If thou canst believe, all things are possible to him that believeth"* (Mark 9:23).

What a promise! God gives believers authority over the affairs of life. As the apostle Paul writes, *"For if by one man's offence death reigned by one; much more they which receive abundance of grace and of the gift of righteousness shall reign in life by one, Jesus*

Christ" (Romans 7:17).

To such a member of the body of Christ, *all* situations can be overcome and nothing is impossible. According to scripture there is nothing in this physical or even spiritual world which can entrap or hinder the believer: *"And we know that all things work together for good to them that love God, to them who are the called according to his purpose"* (Romans 8:28). We also stand on this authority: *"...greater is he that is in you, than he that is in the world"* (1 John 4:4).

When we establish a "believing fellowship" with the Lord, the circumstances and situations of life are swallowed up by the "faith shock-absorbers" of God's Word.

THE DISTINCTION

Many still ask, "What is believing? And what is the difference between belief and faith?"

Believing is what you see, say, feel and think on the inside. Just as in physical science there is both *potential* and *kinetic* energy. So it is with faith and believing.

- Faith is active or energy in motion.
- Believing is passive or energy at rest.

I like to compare the two factors to an iceberg.

Research reveals that only ten percent of an iceberg is seen and the other ninety percent lies beneath the surface of the water.

Faith in God is the part which is visible—like the portion of the iceberg which is exposed above the surface of the water. Believing is what you don't see—it's underneath the water line.

> **BELIEVING IS WHAT YOU DON'T SEE — IT'S UNDERNEATH THE WATER LINE.**

INSIDE AGREEMENT

To believe a particular truth means you are established in what you declare. There is absolutely no doubt, fear, hesitation, wavering or shadow of uncertainty. Your "insides" are united in agreement concerning the matter.

When I refer to "insides," I mean four primary things: (1) your feelings, (2) your thoughts, (3) your "unheard" sayings (what you say to yourself), and (4) your "seeings" (inward images, self esteem/regard).

As a result of this unity, you become relaxed, even casual regarding your belief. The struggle is behind you and you experience a state of peace and rest.

The external demonstration regarding your belief is what we call faith in action. When belief has been established, your steps are not the result of being "told" what to do, they come from you, not someone else.

Any response associated with believing can be considered faith—including our thoughts, feelings, inner voices and images.

FROM YOUR HEART

Until you speak or take action, no one really knows what you actually believe concerning any matter. Jesus says, *"for the tree is known by his fruit"* (Matthew 12:33).

What manifests in your life is a result of what is in your heart—what you see, say, feel and think on the inside (Matthew 15:10-20; Proverbs 23:7). God's Son declares: *"...for out of the abundance of the heart the mouth speaketh"* (Matthew 12:34).

Since my words and actions are an outgrowth of what I believe, if I want strong faith I must first acquire strong belief. It all begins with my heart.

Believing is developed through:

- **Preaching** (1 Corinthians 15:11; Romans 10:14-15; 1 Corinthians 1:17-24).
- **Meditation** (Genesis 24:63; Joshua 1:8).
- **Association** (Acts 9:26-28).
- **Impartation** (Acts 8:4-6,13; 2 Timothy 1:6).
- **Visualization** (John 4:48; Genesis 15:1-6).

What is preached to you, what you meditate upon, what you associate with on a regular basis, what is imparted unto you and what you see becomes an integral part of you. At the finish line of this process you have what is called believing.

Attending a Bible-teaching church, listening to tapes or CD's, associating with other Christians, *doing* the Word of God and seeing people experience the power of Jehovah will produce and nurture "believing" in your life.

> **BELIEVING IS NOT A PROCESS, RATHER THE END RESULT OF A PROCESS.**

It results from being open and constantly exposed to the message—allowing uninhibited access and entrance into your consciousness and thinking.

Believing is not a process, rather the *end result* of a process.

MANIFESTATIONS DO NOT LIE

In our dealings with the secular world, faith and believing may not mean much, but when addressing spiritual matters, whether of God or Satan, believing is directly related to your success or lack thereof.

Triumph in the unseen realm is determined primarily by how much of God's Word we accept and believe. Many people glibly say, "I believe," yet the results of their lives indicate otherwise.

In my experience, *manifestations do not lie!*

What you receive is what you believe. If you receive nothing *from* God, it is because you believe nothing *toward* Him (Romans 14:22). This simple barometer helps us determine where we are in our spiritual walk.

In the past, when I have not received Bible *results*, I re-examined my Bible believing. In every case, I discovered what was lacking—and the cure was to reinforce the truth of God's Word in my heart: *"For with the heart man believeth unto righteousness; and with the mouth confession is made unto salvation"* (Romans 10:10).

IF YOU RECEIVE NOTHING FROM GOD, IT IS BECAUSE YOU BELIEVE NOTHING TOWARD HIM.

The transformation took place by listening to the Word of God aloud—over and over and over again. Whether I say it with my own mouth (Joshua 1:8) or listen to Bible preaching audio resources, I am living proof that faith comes from hearing the Word (Romans 10:17).

THE WORD DESTROYS UNBELIEF

Shortly after Jesus began His public ministry and

miracles began to occur, He returned to His hometown, accompanied by His disciples. When the Sabbath day came, He began to teach in the synagogue and those who heard Him listened in awe.

The critics, however, began to question how a carpenter's son could be rising to such prominence. The Bible records, *"...they were offended at him"* (Mark 6:3).

As a result of their disbelief, *"...he could there do no mighty work, save that he laid his hands upon a few sick folk, and healed them"* (v.5).

What was the Lord's reaction to their unbelief? He *"Went round the villages teaching"* (v.6).

Instruction in the Word is the remedy for those who doubt (2 Timothy 3:15-16).

AGAINST ALL HOPE

The level of believing reached by Abraham is amazing. Even though he was about 100 years old, God told him he and Sarah would conceive a child—and he *believed!*

Paul writes about this in his letter to the church in Rome, saying, *"For the promise, that he should be the heir of the world, was not to Abraham, or to his seed, through the law, but through the righteousness of faith"* (Romans 4:13).

Abraham never forgot the covenant God made with him. As a result, *"...against hope* [he] *believed in hope, that he might become the father of many nations, according to that which was spoken, So shall thy seed be"* (v.18).

What was Abraham's secret? He walked in total belief. The Bible says, *"And being not weak in faith, he considered not his own body now dead, when he was about an hundred years old, neither yet the deadness of Sarah's womb"* (v.19).

WHAT WAS ABRAHAM'S SECRET? HE WALKED IN TOTAL BELIEF.

Talk about a hopeless situation! He and Sarah were double-dead as far as being parents, yet these negatives Abraham *"considered not."*

Regardless of the circumstances, his believing prevailed and overpowered the "deadness."

A TIME FOR VICTORY

The ultimate source of belief which will extricate you from life's most difficult circumstances is the infallible, immutable Word of God.

When you reach the place where you trust *only* the Word, victory begins to replace defeat. As a direct result of Bible believing and confidence in the Almighty:

- ■ *You'll have God's protection.* *"A thousand shall fall at thy side, and ten thousand at thy right hand; but it shall not come nigh thee"* (Psalm 91:7).
- ■ *You'll have God's direction.* *"Thy word is a lamp unto my feet, and a light unto my path"* (Psalm 119:105).
- ■ *You'll have God's affection.* Jesus says, *"If a man love me, he will keep my words: and my Father will love him, and we will come unto him, and make our abode with him"* (John 14:23).

FOUR FOUNDATIONS OF BELIEF

It is a divine principle that the more we believe, the more we receive. However, you may ask, "Exactly what should I believe?"

Let me answer that from personal experience. In studying God's Word, there are four important directives which have become highly active in my daily life. Let me share them with you:

1. I must believe the Bible is God talking to me.

This is not a book written for my intellectual stimulation or enjoyment. God's Holy Word is the Father talking intimately to you and me—and when I want to hear from Him, I turn to what He says (Romans

31

15:4; 2 Timothy 3:14-17; 1 Peter 1:19-21).

Scripture speaks to the deepest parts of my life. *"For the word of God is quick, and powerful, and sharper than any twoedged sword, piercing even to the dividing asunder of soul and spirit, and of the joints and marrow, and is a discerner of the thoughts and intents of the heart"* (Hebrews 4:12).

THE BIBLE IS GOD'S PERSONAL TESTIMONY CONCERNING HIMSELF, HIS WORLD, HIS LOVE AND HIS WAYS.

The Bible is God's personal testimony concerning Himself, His world, His love and His ways (John 3:8-13; John 3:31-36; I John 5:6-11).

Again, I *must* believe that through scripture, the Almighty is speaking directly to me. There is unlimited power available to any person who accepts this truth.

2. I must believe in the name of Jesus Christ.

God the Father has highly exalted the name of Jesus and has given Him a name which is above every name in existence (Philippians 2:9-11; Ephesians 1:21-23).

To every person who will receive Him, God gives redemption through the name of His Son. In fact, it is the only way: *"Neither is there salvation in any other: for there is none other name under heaven given among men, whereby we must be saved"* (Acts 4:12).

The name of Jesus:

- ***Gives access to the Father*** (John 14:12-14; 15:16; 16:23-24).
- ***Gives power over Satan and his demons*** (Luke 10:17-19; Acts 3:1-10; Acts 16:16-18).
- ***Is ours for every situation, under all circumstances or conditions*** (Colossians 3:17).

However, if we do not have faith in the name of Jesus (Acts 3:16) we forfeit by default all the victory and power inherent in His wonderful name.

John the apostle declares, *"These things have I written unto you that believe on the name of the son of God; that ye may know that ye have eternal life, and that ye may believe on the name of the son of God"* (John 5:13).

This is not a suggestion; it is a *requirement*.

3. I must believe what I say will come to pass.

Churches are filled with members who constantly talk doubt and unbelief—yet somehow think their lives are pleasing to God. What a mistake! Every believer needs to know that both their words and their salvation are equally important (Mark 11:22-24; Job 22:28; Joshua 1:8; 2 Corinthians 4:13; Romans 10:8-10).

Because of my salvation, my words should be

different (Matthew 12:34-37).

Paul reminds us of this truth as he writes: *"Howbeit we speak wisdom among them that are perfect: yet not the wisdom of this world, nor of the princes of this world, that come to nought: But we speak the wisdom of God in a mystery, even the hidden wisdom, which God ordained before the world unto our glory"* (1 Corinthians 2:6-7).

A few verses later, the apostle adds, *"Which things also we speak, not in the words which man's wisdom teacheth, but which the Holy Ghost teacheth; comparing spiritual things with spiritual"* (v.13).

It is clear from these scriptures—and many more like them—that my conversation should be a reflection of my identification with God. Not only do I have a brand new heart, I also have a new tongue. Yes, *"all things have become new"* (2 Corinthians 5:17)—including my speech. Since God's Word is on my lips, I now have a Christ-centered vocabulary!

If I profess to trust in the Word, I must also believe that what I say (consistent with scripture) will come to pass. Jesus is an example of this as He declares, *"...the words that I speak unto you, they* [the words] *are spirit, and they are life"* (John 6:63).

Believing "What I say will come into reality," will eliminate many of the problems you face. I am convinced the spiritual health many Christians seek can be found in this powerful Master principle. Satan would love for us to be totally ignorant in this area.

4. I must believe in prayer.

God has given prayer as a means of fellowship and communication with Him. It is our direct link to Heaven and the throne of God—and an awesome privilege.

Let me encourage you to cherish prayer more than any earthly activity—otherwise Satan will take advantage. Remember, this earth is his arena of operation

> **PRAYER...IS OUR DIRECT LINK TO HEAVEN AND THE THRONE OF GOD.**

(Revelation 12:6-17). It is where he kills, steals and destroys (John 10:10). We are warned to *"Be sober, be vigilant; because your adversary the devil, as a roaring lion, walketh about, seeking whom he may devour"* (1 Peter 5:7).

A prayerless believer is a *powerless* believer.

Constant, unbroken communion with the Lord will keep you in a state of readiness. It is the medium through which the name of Jesus is declared—and it allows the blood of Christ to shine in all of its cleansing, righteous, wonder-working power.

A primary reason prayer is such an indescribable experience is because angels move and flow with us as we fellowship with the Father (Acts 12:5-16; Luke 22:41-45).

As I frequently tell my own congregation, "Prayer will get you there."

UNLOCKING GOD'S STOREHOUSE

Have you experienced the power of believing? Have you built a strong foundation for your faith?

Make certain you are totally convinced God's Word is not only true, but that it is speaking directly to you. Declare the name of Jesus and believe what you say will come into reality. When these are linked with an active prayer life, God graciously unlocks His storehouse of abundance and blessing.

CHAPTER 3

SEVEN REASONS
TO LIVE BY FAITH

Without question, the greatest existence available to any human being is living by faith.

It is the means by which we receive salvation. Scripture declares, *"For by grace are ye saved through faith; and that not of yourselves: it is the gift of God"* (Ephesians 2:8).

From the moment you repent of your sin and start walking as a born again follower of Christ, you should take advantage of every opportunity to develop the strength of your believing.

Let's take a look at what the Bible says concerning the power of faith. After detailing the role of faith in the lives of great men and women such as Enoch, Noah, Abraham, Sarah, Joseph, Moses and more, we read that space would not permit the stories of those, *"Who through faith subdued kingdoms, wrought righteousness, obtained promises, stopped the mouths of lions, Quenched the violence of fire, escaped the edge of the sword, out of weakness were made strong, waxed valiant in fight, turned to flight the armies of the aliens. Women received their dead raised to life again: and others were tortured, not accepting deliverance; that they might obtain a better resurrection"* (Hebrews 11:33-35).

The fantastic testimonies of miracles as a result of faith fill pages of the New Testament. In fact, if the Book of Acts were being written today, there would be millions of additional accounts to be added. As a minister of the Gospel, I have personally experienced, many amazing manifestations of this God-given treasure.

THE "FAITH LIFE" IS BASICALLY LIVING BY YOUR ACTIONS AND SPEAKING BASED UPON THE WORD OF GOD.

A FAMILY OF FAITH

After careful study of scripture and putting it into practice all of my adult life, I can safely say the "faith life" is basically living by your actions and speaking based upon the Word of God.

Here is good news. If you are born again you have at least what I call "John 3:16 faith." Then, as members of the family of God, we all have the *"same spirit of*

38

faith" (2 Corinthians 4:13).

There is even more. According to the Bible, you are of *"the household of faith"* (Galatians 6:10).

Some ask, "If it takes faith to be a Christian, where does the initial portion come from?"

The Bible tells us, *"God hath dealt to every man the measure of faith"* (Romans 12:3). It grows and develops through the hearing of His Word (Romans 10:17).

We are also told, *"...the righteousness of God is revealed from faith to faith"* (Romans 1:17). It would be impossible to progress from one faith to the next unless we have a certain amount to begin with.

AFTER THE CROSS

It is important to consider that most of the contents of Matthew, Mark, Luke and John were written to men who were not born again. At the time of Jesus' earthly ministry, people did not have the nature of God within them. Only in the final chapters of these four books—after Jesus had been raised from the dead—was He addressing men and women who were in the family of God as we know it today.

This is vital to understand since many contemporary believers mistakenly see themselves *before* the cross rather than after.

In the Gospels, Jesus constantly uses phrases such

ANDRÉ GORHAM

as "If ye had faith," "Have faith," "Where is your faith?" and "O ye of little faith."

However, when you turn to the book of Acts and beyond, you do not see one commandment to "have faith." Why not? Because from Acts forward, the Bible is written to believers.

When you read the letters penned to the churches you will notice that each epistle, whether by Paul, Peter, James or John, was addressed to those who already believed in God the Father, but who had accepted Jesus Christ as their Lord and Savior.

Personally, I see myself:

- ***Through the eyes of the cross*** (Galatians 2:20).
- ***As a son of God*** (1 John 3:1-2).
- ***As a joint-heir with Christ*** (Romans 8:17).
- ***As a believer*** (2 Corinthians 6:16-18).

I am not searching for faith—praise God, it's already mine!

EQUIPPED FOR GREATNESS

We have the capability, means and wherewithal to have all the faith necessary to do and be whatever the Bible commands. I get excited when I think of how the Father has made us *"partakers of the inheritance of the saints in light"* (Colossians 1:12).

40

We have been equipped by God to receive everything He promised.

It's sad to realize many believers have never invested enough time to discover *who they are* and *what they have* in Christ Jesus. This is a must. You should study at length the letters of the apostle Paul and other portions of the New Testament because these books are addressed to you—the believer. They speak to the person who is now *"alive unto God"* (Romans 6:11).

You will learn of your Son-ship, your authority in Christ, how to defeat Satan and the marvelous love of the Father toward you. In addition, you'll understand your dominion in the earth because of what Jesus, our Lord and Savior, accomplished on the cross and after His resurrection.

> **YOUR FAITH WILL COINCIDE WITH THE WORD AND YOU WILL BECOME A SPIRITUAL "TOUR DE FORCE."**

Once you receive these Bible truths through faith, you will go about doing good and healing those who are oppressed of the devil. Your faith will coincide with the Word and you will become a spiritual "tour de force."

SPEAKING WITH POWER

When I say *"I can do all things through Christ,"* it

41

is because Philippians 4:13 tells me so. I live *"by every word that proceedeth out of the mouth of God"* (Matthew 4:4).

This is the meaning of living by faith.

In the garden of Eden, Adam named the animals and whatever he called them, that is what they were forever named (Genesis 2:19-20). Then, when God brought the woman, Adam immediately said, *"This is now bone of my bones and flesh of my flesh"* (Genesis 2:23).

ADAM LEARNED THE POWER OF THE SPOKEN WORD FROM HIS FATHER, GOD.

Adam learned the power of the spoken word from his Father, God.

Once you discover the nature of your relationship with your Heavenly Father you will speak with confidence and authority. Your words will determine your future because they will coincide with the Word of God (John 6:61-63). You will have what you say (Mark 11:23), and when you decree a thing it will be established unto you (Job 22:28).

Why will you speak with such power? Because you believe! (2 Corinthians 4:13).

WHY LIVE BY FAITH?

Considering these truths, let me share seven reasons

why we should live by our faith:

1. Living by faith pleases God.

This is the "substance" given to us by the Father so we can bring joy and delight to Him. As scripture declares, *"...without faith it is impossible to please him: for he that cometh to God must believe that he is, and that he is a rewarder of them that diligently seek him"* (Hebrews 11:6 KJV).

2. Living by faith glorifies the Father.

Never forget Abraham. In the natural, it looked as though his seed would never produce a child—much less a nation. Yet, *"He staggered not at the promise of God through unbelief; but was strong in faith, giving glory to God; And being fully persuaded that, what he had promised, he was able also to perform"* (Romans 4:20-21).

God received all the praise and honor.

3. Living by faith is the victory which overcomes the world.

Heroes of military history have conquered nations, even continents, yet not one can say, "I have triumphed over the world and its system of operation."

As believers, however, we can make such a claim: *"For whatsoever is born of God overcometh the world:*

and this is the victory that overcometh the world, even our faith" (1 John 5:4).

4. Living by faith is the Father's way of making provision for His children.

The Lord looks after His own. *"For the promise, that he should be the heir of the world, was not to Abraham, or to his seed, through the law, but through the righteousness of faith"* (Romans 4:13).

5. Living by faith is how we resist Satan.

After describing the devil as an adversary prowling the earth searching for whom he may devour, Peter tells us we can resist him, by being *"stedfast in the faith"* (1 Peter 5:9).

6. Living by faith is a unique characteristic of the children of God.

Those who have never accepted Jesus as their personal Savior cannot claim to live by faith. Why? Because the Word tells us, *"For ye are all the children of God by faith in Christ Jesus"* (Galatians 3:26). *"...for we walk by faith and not by sight"* (2 Corinthians 5:7).

7. Faith in God accomplishes the impossible.

Regarding the birth of Jesus, the angel Gabriel tells

Mary, *"For with God nothing shall be impossible"* (Luke 1:37). What seems out of the question with man, is possible through faith in God.

In many areas of life, despite our best efforts, we often fall short. This is true because success in one realm of life does not necessarily translate into accomplishment in another. For example, a person may achieve great financial success, yet fail at family matters. Or, an individual may be an outstanding father

> ### WHAT SEEMS OUT OF THE QUESTION WITH MAN, IS POSSIBLE THROUGH FAITH IN GOD.

or mother, yet never discover the ability to pay their bills on time.

To some desires, we say, "impossible"—meaning there is no way it will ever occur. To our human minds it is unreasonable, even *irrational* to think it could ever happen. This is when we need to move into another dimension and see our faith in God shine like the brightness of the noonday sun.

In Genesis, the angel that visited Abraham and Sarah informed them that with God all things are possible. It was this truth that catapulted Abraham and Sarah into the God-pleasing faith that produced a son in Sarah's previously barren womb.

A FAMILY TRAGEDY

I know what it means to have faith in "The God of the Impossible."

When our oldest son was about eighteen months old, he suffered severe burns on his right hand. We were just beginning to raise a family when this tragedy occurred.

Immediately we rushed our son to the hospital where we were told he had second and third degree burns. They assigned outstanding physicians to the case—including a renowned specialist from a burn center. He informed us, "Unless we operate immediately, you son will likely lose the full use of his right hand. At best, as he gets older, his hand won't be able to close."

> **IMMEDIATELY WE RUSHED OUR SON TO THE HOSPITAL WHERE WE WERE TOLD HE HAD SECOND AND THIRD DEGREE BURNS.**

Despite the great medical facilities, the prognosis from the team of doctors was bleak. We were informed that a skin graft "may or may not take" and there would probably be several surgeries over a period of time.

Of course, my wife and I began to pray.

Even at that time in our lives, we knew enough about faith, prayer and the Word of God to produce a different outcome. We began thanking God in advance for a complete healing—and believing that our son would have full use of his right hand.

> ### WE BEGAN THANKING GOD IN ADVANCE FOR A COMPLETE HEALING - AND BELIEVING THAT OUR SON WOULD HAVE FULL USE OF HIS RIGHT HAND.

A DECISION OF FAITH

Please understand, I have nothing but the highest admiration for medical science and the wonderful physicians and surgeons who make life easier for millions around the world. I knew the doctors and nurses were for us, not against us.

However, at this moment, I stood on the Word spoken to the children of Israel, *"I am the Lord that healeth thee"* (Exodus 15:26)..

I knew and believed this before this accident and during it—both for myself and for my young son. Believing the Lord for healing was nothing new. God had done it for me and my family before and I knew He would do it again.

I thanked the burn specialist for his help, then, after making sure that I was not missing God or being foolish, I informed him, "Sir, we have decided not to have the surgery."

"SIR, WE HAVE DECIDED NOT TO HAVE THE SURGERY."

My wife and I were in agreement. We would stand upon God's Word concerning our son's severely burned hand.

THE MASTER SURGEON

Today, many years later, my son has full use of his right hand—and is an excellent basketball player At the time, we wondered if the potential emotional and psychological trauma would cause him to use his left hand, yet this did not happen.

Over the years, several people who have been burned, noticed the scar on his hand and asked, "Did he have surgery?"

I respond with a simple "No"—with the private knowledge that faith in God had accomplished the impossible.

WHAT A WAY TO LIVE!

One of the most profound statements in both the Old and New Testaments is: *"The just shall live by faith"* (Romans 1:17; Habakkuk 2:4). What a vivid contrast to those who live according to the world system—with all its carnality and flesh.

As sons and daughters of the Most High, we *"walk by faith, not by sight"* (2 Corinthians 5:7).

What a God-given, glorious privilege!

CHAPTER 4

"I BELIEVE IN GOD"

Y ou can search from Genesis to Revelation, yet you won't find a denominational tag. Being named Presbyterian, Lutheran or Methodist is the result of doctrinal divisions and man's desires to be "exclusive."

In the Bible we are simply classified as *believers.* It is a title of honor which indicates we have chosen to believe the Word of God—as opposed to something or someone else.

This is extremely significant! Actually, biblical "unbelief" can be defined as embracing anything other than what is indicated in scripture. When a Christian says he is "a believer," this is more than a casual phrase used to identify a religious affiliation. It means we have denounced, rejected and totally abandoned all other opinions about certain issues. In their place we have chosen to stand on God's Word in at least one particular area—salvation by faith in Christ.

A NEVER-ENDING TRUST

In many religious circles, saying "I believe God" is nothing more than a cliché. This becomes all too evident when the tests and trials associated with actual Bible faith exposes a person's "believing" as nothing more than blatant skepticism and unbelief.

How refreshing it is to meet a man or woman of faith who, in the midst of a tragedy, can say, *"Greater is he that is in me than he that is in the world"* (1 John 4:4).

> **IF WE TRULY TRUST GOD, HE WILL BE GLORIFIED AS THE RESULT OF OUR UNSWERVING BELIEF.**

If we truly trust God, He will be glorified as the result of our unswerving belief.

The world may not understand, yet the Lord knows. For *"God hath chosen the foolish things of the world to confound the wise; and God hath chosen the weak things of the world to confound the things which are mighty; And base things of the world, and things which are despised, hath God chosen, yea, and things which are not, to bring to nought things that are: That no flesh should glory in his presence"* (1 Corinthians 1:27-29).

However, to those who have been redeemed, it is written, *"He that glorieth, let him glory in the Lord"* (v.31).

DANGER AHEAD!

If you really want to know what it means to believe in God, read the story of Paul being escorted by soldiers along with other "criminals" to Rome. As they traveled, Paul spoke to those in charge of the vessel, saying: *"Sirs, I perceive that this voyage will be with hurt and much damage, not only of the lading and the ship, but also of our lives"* (Acts 27:10).

Despite this warning, obviously coming from within Paul's spirit, the Bible tells us, *"Nevertheless the centurion believed the master and the owner of the ship, more than those things which were spoken by Paul"* (v.11). They sailed on.

A PRAYER OF FAITH

At this point I believe Paul began seeking God in earnest for the safety of the crew and himself. Satan would have been delighted to destroy the apostle, or to limit his future ministry activities. However, I am convinced it was Paul's prayer of faith which made the difference. He was no fool—and certainly not ignorant of Satan's devices (2 Corinthians 2:11).

As they sailed along the shore near the island of Crete, suddenly a wind of hurricane force arose and the ship took such a violent beating they, in fear, began to toss the cargo overboard (Acts 27:18).

Then, *"when neither sun nor stars in many days appeared, and no small tempest lay on us, all hope that we should be saved was then taken away"* (Acts 27:20).

SUPERNATURAL HOPE

The situation was desperate—especially since celestial navigation was essential on the open sea. These seasoned veterans of the oceans had obviously resigned themselves to the mercy of the storm. They were afraid—and justifiably so.

Before the tempest these same men were confident of a safe journey (Acts 27:12-14). Paul, on the other hand, had a hope which was supernatural in origin. He was trusting Someone other than the "tempestuous wind."

At the height of the storm, an angel appeared to the apostle and said, *"Fear not, Paul; thou must be brought before Caesar: and, lo, God hath given thee all them that sail with thee"* (Acts 27:24).

Paul immediately gathered the frightened crew around him and told them not to worry, Then he made this declaration: *"I believe God"* (Acts 27:25).

What a statement!

STRONG IN THE LORD

Where did Paul obtain such unwavering faith? He possessed it because of his dramatic encounter with God on the road to Damascus and had been strengthened by his walk with God and his knowledge of the Word of God (2 Timothy 4:16-17) as he preached Christ to the known world.

Paul was not attempting to be a "positive thinker" in the midst of a crisis. He actually believed *"that it shall be even as it was told me"* (v.25).

When you have total trust in what God says, you are not influenced by either good weather or bad. Paul was not trying to be brave in himself, rather *"he was strong in the Lord and in the power of His might"* (Ephesians 6:10).

BEYOND EMOTION

Believing God is not a feeling, an emotion or some temporary euphoria. It is a state of being which transcends merely "knowing" from an intellectual standpoint. You are certain God will do something according to His Word and are filled with an

> BELIEVING GOD IS NOT A FEELING OF EMOTION OR SOME TEMPORARY EUPHORIA.

assurance and certainty that all is well.

The conviction is so "dense and thick" you cannot be swayed. It is a "believing" stronger than any tempest.

This was Paul's glorious condition during this raging storm. It is also what kept him and those who traveled with him alive (Acts 27:24).

UNWAVERING ASSURANCE

From this example, we know that to "believe God" is more than being comforted until the winds die down. Instead of a struggle—as so many would have you believe—it is a posture of faith, a stance of unwavering assurance.

> WE KNOW THAT TO "BELIEVE GOD" IS MORE THAN BEING COMFORTED UNTIL THE WINDS DIE DOWN.

Is it possible for you to have this extraordinary strength? Can you operate on such a level in our contemporary society? Will the Lord honor you in the same way as He honored the apostle Paul? YES! YES! AND ONE THOUSAND TIMES YES!

In writing to the believers in Corinth, Paul says, *"I believed, therefore have I spoken; we also believe, and therefore speak"* (2 Corinthians 4:13).

Can you make the same bold statement? Here's

how it works in my own life:

- I *confess* the Word of God because I *believe* the Word.
- I *believe* the Word because I have *received* the Word.
- The *faith* I have from the Word has come through *hearing* the Word.

We don't just wake up one morning automatically believing God. It takes being *bathed* in the Word.

My passion in life is to "get me in the Word and the Word in me." As Jesus proclaims, *"If ye abide in me, and my words abide in you, ye shall ask what ye will, and it shall be done unto you"* (John 15:7).

> **YOU DON'T JUST WAKE UP ONE MORNING AUTOMATICALLY BELIEVING GOD. IT TAKES BEING BATHED IN THE WORD.**

BELIEVING BRINGS LIFE

You don't need a Greek lexicon to understand God is extremely serious concerning us believing in Him. Jesus told the disciples before leaving to raise Lazarus from the dead that He was *"glad for* [their] *sakes that I was not there, to the intent ye may believe"* (John 11:15).

57

ANDRÉ GORHAM

Scripture also records, *"And many other signs truly did Jesus in the presence of His disciples, which are not written in this book; But these are written, that ye might believe that Jesus is the Christ, the Son of God; and that believing ye might have life through His name"* (John 20:30-31).

GIVE YOURSELF TOTALLY

Let me encourage you to stop struggling with believing (Romans 15:3-4). Delve into the Word and develop your faith in areas where you are weak and undernourished. There is so much in scripture to build your faith.

Follow the advice Paul gives to young Timothy: *"...give attendance to reading, to exhortation, to doctrine...Meditate upon these things; give thyself wholly to them; that thy profiting may appear to all"* (1 Timothy 4:13,15).

> IF LIFE IS A TEST, I AM GLAD THAT WITH THE WORD OF GOD IT IS AN "OPEN BOOK" TEST!

How else will you believe? Surely not just during a crisis. Paul believed God *before, during* and *after* the storm. He did not change, nor did he hesitate. This missionary-evangelist was full of the persuasion which only comes from truly knowing God.

A PERFECT WORK

If life is a test, I am glad that with the Word of God it is an "open book" test! Now that this divine knowledge has come into your life, circumstances and trials only expose where you are spiritually, because the trying of your faith works patience. Knowing this, *"...let patience have her perfect work, that ye may be perfect and entire, wanting nothing"* (James 1:4).

Thank God for unmovable faith. To quote the psalmist, *"...the man that feareth the Lord, that delighteth greatly in His commandments...shall not be afraid of evil tidings: his heart is fixed, trusting in the Lord"* (Psalm 112:1,7).

I pray you are able to say with me, "I believe God"—and mean it with every fiber of your being.

CHAPTER 5

UNDERSTANDING SPIRITUAL BLESSINGS

Many of the letters written by the apostle Paul were to correct some doctrinal error or heresy in the early church. His letter to the believers at Ephesus, however, was totally different. It was for edification, to expand the thinking of his readers regarding God's eternal purpose and the high goals He has set for His children.

Paul's opening greeting includes these insightful words: *"Blessed be the God and Father of our Lord Jesus Christ, Who hath blessed us with all spiritual blessings in heavenly places in Christ"* (Ephesians 1:3).

This is wonderful news, but what exactly are *"spiritual blessings"*? And it is only natural to ask, "If we have been favored in such a manner, how can I make these blessings a material reality in my personal life?

THE "UNSEEN"

Contrary to what many think, the term *spiritual* does not mean "unreal." Instead, it is a synonym of the word "unseen." Therefore, if we were to paraphrase Ephesians 1:3 with this definition in mind, I believe we would glean a greater appreciation for these "in Christ" blessings. "Blessed be the God and Father of our Lord Jesus Christ, who hath blessed us with all *unseen* blessings in heavenly places in Christ."

This view is made clear in Paul's letter to the Corinthians as he writes, *"While we look not at the things which are seen, but at the things which are not seen: for the things which are seen are temporal; but the things which are not seen are eternal"* (2 Corinthians 4:18).

These words remind me how, as a believer, I do not need to see what is physical or tangible in order to believe it is real. Remember, *"...we walk by faith, not by sight"* (2 Corinthians 5:7). To paraphrase, "...we walk by what we *see* on the inside of us, not by what we *see* on the outside." Basically, our steps are the result of *believing*.

SEEING THE INVISIBLE

As a member of the body of Christ, the eyes by which I see are not natural but spiritual—or *unseen*.

This is because, *"God is a Spirit: and they that worship Him must worship Him in spirit and in truth"* (John 4:24).

Think of it this way: God is an *Unseen* Being and those who worship Him must do so in that unseen part of themselves—and in truth.

Thousands of years ago, Moses, by faith, led the children of Israel toward the promised land because he heard the inaudible, saw the invisible and did the impossible. The Bible records how Moses *"endured, as seeing Him Who is invisible"* (Hebrews 11:27).

> **MOSES...HEARD THE INAUDIBLE, SAW THE INVISIBLE AND DID THE IMPOSSIBLE.**

As believers, we should do no less.

HOW IT HAPPENS

Earlier, we spoke of the miracle of Abraham and Sarah giving birth to a son in their old age. When we look behind the scenes, we learn how that which is spiritual (unseen) becomes reality.

What God promised Abraham early in his walk was a blessing he couldn't visualize at the time. It was not physical, nor was it in his possession.

When we read the story closely, Abraham had to *do* something to take what God initially promised and make it tangible. This is important since if we do the things Abraham did, then we can receive the things Abraham received.

EIGHT REASONS FOR BLESSINGS

Abraham was not made righteous by his works, but by his faith. The Bible tells us, *"For if Abraham were justified by works, he hath whereof to glory; but not before God"* (Romans 4:2). What does the scripture say? *"Abraham believed God, and it was counted unto him for righteousness"* (v.3).

If we are the children of Abraham, it's time to follow his pattern. Paul counsels us to *"walk in the steps of that faith of our father Abraham"* (Romans 4:12).

Exactly how did Abraham obtain these spiritual, unseen blessings? There are eight reasons:

1. He believed God's promises.

The Lord made a covenant with Abraham, saying, *"I will make of thee a great nation, and I will bless thee, and make thy name great; and thou shalt be a blessing: And I will bless them that bless thee, and curse him that curseth thee: and in thee shall all families of the earth be blessed"* (Genesis 12:2-3).

Not only did Abraham follow God's command, the Bible says, *"he believed in the Lord"* (Genesis 15:6).

2. He was strong in faith.

God instructed Abraham, to *"Lift up now thine eyes, and look from the place where thou art northward, and southward, and eastward, and westward: For all the land which thou seest, to thee will I give it, and to thy seed for ever"* (Genesis 13:14-15).

By faith, the "Father of Nations" took his wife and all the possessions they had accumulated and *"removed his tent, and came and dwelt in the plain of Mamre, which is in Hebron"* (v.18).

Why was Abraham willing to leave his home in the Ur of the Chaldees for the unknown? Because he *"was strong in faith"* (Romans 4:20).

3. He obeyed the Lord.

Abraham's adventure with God can be characterized as one of unmitigated obedience. The Bible says, *"...by faith Abraham, when he was called to go out into a place which he should after receive for an inheritance, obeyed; and he went out, not knowing whither he went"* (Hebrews 11:8).

The Lord Himself testifies concerning Abraham's

> ABRAHAM'S ADVENTURE WITH GOD CAN BE CHARACTERIZED AS ONE OF UNMITIGATED OBEDIENCE.

willingness to follow, as He states, *"...for I know him that he will command his children after him, and they shall keep the way of the Lord, to do justice and judgement"* (Genesis 18:19).

Many believers erroneously think our blessings are pre-determined by God. This is not always the case. The Lord is ready and waiting to shower us with abundance, but it is in response to our obedience. According to God's Word, *"If they obey and serve Him, they shall spend their days in prosperity, and their years in pleasures. But if they obey not, they shall perish by the sword, and they shall die without knowledge"* (Job 36:11-12).

4. He spoke the words of God.

Abraham made certain his words coincided with God's. Even though the Lord revealed the marvelous plan for his future, it was Abraham's responsibility to *agree* with God and confirm what the Lord had said about his situation.

We must do likewise. As the psalmist prays, *"Let the words of my mouth and the meditation of my heart be acceptable in thy sight, O Lord, my strength and my redeemer"* (Psalm 19:4).

Language contrary to scripture is counter-productive to our spiritual well-being. Let what you say be in total alliance with what is spoken in the Word.

5. He did not falter.

Through the years of famine, family quarrels and even the destruction of Sodom and Gomorrah, Abraham's trust and belief in God remained solid as a rock. He may have made personal mistakes, yet his faith never faltered (Romans 4:20).

------■------

ABRAHAM'S TRUST AND BELIEF IN GOD REMAINED SOLID AS A ROCK.

6. He exercised patience.

Abraham not only stepped out in belief, he continued to follow in God's ways.

Using this great hero of the faith as an example, the writer of Hebrews says, *"And we desire that every one of you do shew the same diligence to the full assurance of hope unto the end: that you be not slothful, but followers of them who through faith and patience inherit the promises"* (Hebrews 11:12).

When the Almighty made His eternal promise to Abraham, since there was no one greater to administer the oath, *"He sware by Himself, saying, Surely blessing I will bless thee, and multiplying I will multiply thee. And so, after he*[Abraham] *had patiently endured, he obtained the promise"* (vv.13-15).

Patience is an unseen fruit of the Spirit.

7. He remained totally convinced in God's ability.

What a test of faith it was for Abraham to offer his "miracle son" Isaac on an altar of sacrifice. Yet, that is exactly what God required him to do (Genesis 22:2).

After traveling by donkey with two of his servants and Isaac for three days to the place the Lord directed him, Abraham *"took the wood of the burnt offering, and laid it upon Isaac his son"* Genesis 22:6).

Isaac spoke up: "Father, the fire and wood are here, but where is the lamb for the burnt offering?"

"MY SON, GOD WILL PROVIDE."

With total assurance, Abraham answered, *"My Son, God will provide"* (Genesis 22:8).

What faith! At that moment an angel from heaven called out, "Abraham, do not lay a hand on that boy"— *"...for now I know that thou fearest God, seeing thou hast not withheld thy son, thine only son from me"*(Genesis 22:12).

Behind them, caught in a thicket, was the ram God provided for the sacrifice.

To the end of his days, Abraham was *"fully persuaded that what He* [God] *had promised He was able also to perform"* (Romans 4:21).

8. He gave God the glory.

At every major turning point in his life, Abraham

took the time to worship the Lord. After receiving his original call from God, *"...there he builded an altar unto the Lord"* (Genesis 12:8). It happened again at Hebron, where he erected another altar (Genesis 13:18) and worshiped the Almighty.

What was his first action after God rescued Isaac from the sacrificial fire? Abraham consecrated the ground, calling the place *"Jehovahjireh"* (Genesis 22:14)—which means "The Lord will Provide."

Throughout his long life, Abraham was *"strong in faith, giving glory to God"* (Romans 4:20).

Friend, today I am praying you will use these same unseen forces—from believing to worship—to receive unexpected spiritual blessings. I know you will rejoice and give God all glory, honor and praise!

CHAPTER 6

A LIVING FAITH

You can travel the globe and find people bowing before golden shrines, worshiping colorful icons and placing their hands on objects called "sacred."

What separates Christianity from the world's religions? Our belief and trust is not in the Christ who remains on the cross, but in the resurrected, living Jesus. Hallelujah! He is alive—and so is our faith!

The object of our belief is a Person: *"For ye are all the children of God by faith in Christ Jesus"* (Galatians 3:26).

In case you have not met Him, I want to personally introduce you to the risen Lord. In the process we will answer these three vital questions:

1. What is Jesus now?
2. Who is Jesus now?
3. Where is Jesus now?

HOW DO YOU SEE HIM?

When believers think of Christ, many have their reference point as the Jesus of the four Gospels. You may visualize a baby wrapped in swaddling clothes, lying in a manger in Bethlehem—or you may see Him walking along the shores of Galilee.

Some may picture Him raising Lazarus from the dead, or casting seven devils out of Mary Magdalene. Perhaps you still think of Jesus as a child, walking the dusty streets of the insignificant Roman garrison town of Nazareth.

My friend, I have some potentially disturbing news for you. The Jesus of the Gospels no longer exists. He died on a Roman cross on Golgotha's hill and was buried in a borrowed tomb. He no longer lives (Acts 4:10-12).

"WHO HAVE I BEEN WORSHIPING ON SUNDAY MORNINGS?"

THE "OLD JESUS"

You may question, "Then who have I been worshiping on Sunday mornings? Who is the Person symbolized on countless paintings and effigies around the world?"

As you are about to discover, that person died and is no more.

72

The image in many believer's minds as they sing worship songs or meditate on Christ is the Jesus *before* the cross–the son of Mary and step-son of Joseph the carpenter. We even envision Jesus as Jewish.

Let me say this as clearly as I can. When Jesus died, someone else rose from the dead—a different person altogether. A New Creation came out of the grave.

- He is no longer from Nazareth.
- He is no longer the son of Mary.
- He is no longer Jewish.
- He is no longer Man—He is God!

ALIVE FOREVERMORE!

Since this is true, you have every right to ask, "Then Who is He? What is He?"

Let's look at how Jesus refers to *Himself* in John's Revelation: *"I am He that liveth, and was dead; and, behold, I am alive forevermore, Amen and have the keys of Hell and of death"* (Revelation 1:18).

This provides insight into this "new" Jesus. We read the story from the accounts in the Gospels, but Who and What is this Person who is "alive forever"? He is Jesus the Resurrected One.

John the Divine saw the following: *"One like unto the Son of man clothed with a garment down to the foot, and girt about the paps with a golden girdle. His head and his hairs were white like wool, as white as snow; and His eyes were as a flame of fire; and His feet like unto fine brass, as if they burned in a furnace; and his voice as the sound of many waters. And He had in His right hand seven stars: and out of His mouth went a sharp twoedged sword: and His countenance was as the sun shineth in his strength"* (Revelation 1:13-16).

John also gives this description concerning the *new* Jesus: *"And I saw Heaven opened, and behold a white horse; and He that sat upon him was called Faithful and True, and in righteousness He doth judge and make war. His eyes were as a flame of fire, and on His head were many crowns and He had a name written, that no man knew but Himself. And He was clothed with a vesture dipped in blood: and His name is called the Word of God...And out of His mouth goeth a sharp sword, that with it He should smite the nations: and He shall rule them with a rod of iron: and He treadeth the winepress of the fierceness and wrath of Almighty God. And He hath on His vesture and on His thigh a name written, KING OF KINGS, AND LORD OF LORDS"* ((Revelation 19:11-14,16).

This is a far cry from the familiar Christmas "babe" lying in a manger.

A NEW CREATION

The apostle Paul was inspired by the Holy Spirit to make this bold pronouncement: *"...though we have*

*known Christ after the flesh, yet now henceforth know
we Him no more"* (2 Corinthians 5:16).

What does this ominous statement mean—that we
would "know Him no more"?

It tells us the man of Galilee is no longer present as
we knew Him. Whatever and
Whoever He was in the flesh
for just over 33 years is gone.

When Paul says, *"...if any
man be in Christ, he is a new
creature"* (2 Corinthians 5:17),
this also includes Jesus, since

> **THE MAN
> OF GALILEE IS
> NO LONGER
> PRESENT AS WE
> KNEW HIM.**

in His own life, *"old things are passed away; behold, all
things are become new"* (v.17).

THE FIRSTBORN

One of the post-resurrection titles given to Jesus is
"Firstborn."

Paul uses this term as he writes that the Son of God
is the *"firstborn among many brethren"* (Romans
8:29).

This is repeated later as Paul gives thanks *"unto the
Father, which hath made us meet to be partakers of the
inheritance of the saints in light: Who hath delivered
us from the power of darkness, and hath translated us
into the kingdom of his dear Son: In whom we have
redemption through his blood, even the forgiveness of*

sins: Who is the image of the invisible God, the firstborn of every creature"(Colossians 1:12-15).

Who is the Firstborn? Jesus—in whom we have salvation through His precious blood.

As Firstborn of *"every* creature" He is also head of every *"new* creature" in Christ. This makes it possible for us to *"put on the new man, which after God is created in righteousness and true holiness"* (Ephesians 4:24).

HEAD OVER ALL THINGS

Because we are redeemed sons and daughters of God we are members of the *"church of the firstborn"* (Hebrews 12:23) of which Jesus is the Head. Remember, God *"hath put all things under his feet, and gave him to be the head over all things to the church"* (Ephesians 1:22).

Paul emphasizes this truth when he writes Christ is the *"head of the body, the church: who is the beginning, the firstborn from the dead; that in all things he might have the preeminence"* (Colossians 1:18).

Jesus was also "born again" after overcoming the sinful satanic nature which caused His death. He had the power to lay down his life and take it up again (John 10:15-18). After three days in the grave and spiritual death He was reborn—with a new spirit and a new nature.

WE ALSO ARISE!

Here's the glorious news. Because Christ rose from the dead, all who come after Him are made like Him. This means if He died, we die—and if He arose, we arise!

We have this blessed assurance: *"Now if we be dead with Christ, we believe that we shall also live with him: Knowing that Christ being raised from the dead dieth no more; death hath no more dominion over him. For in that he died, he died*

IF HE DIED, WE DIE - AND IF HE AROSE, WE ARISE!

unto sin once: but in that he liveth, he iveth unto God. Likewise reckon ye also yourselves to be dead indeed unto sin, but alive unto God through Jesus Christ our Lord" (Romans 6:8-11).

THE RESURRECTED JESUS

One man died and another rose. Jesus of Nazareth was buried and Jesus of Heaven walked out of the tomb. He is very much alive and well! We serve a *resurrected* Jesus—who will return with 10,000 of His saints (Jude 1:14). Yes, He is the One who has a sword coming out of His mouth and shall smite the nations and shall rule them with a rod of iron (Revelation 19:15).

However, this same living Jesus is the Person to

whom blood-bought believers from every nation will one day worship.

In John's Revelation, he looked and heard the voices of angels—ten thousand times ten thousand—circling the throne with the living creatures and elders, singing, *"Worthy is the lamb that was slain to receive power, and riches, and wisdom, and strength, and honour, and glory, and blessing"*(Revelation 5:12).

Then, *"...every creature which is in heaven, and on the earth, and under the earth, and such as are in the sea, and all that are in them, heard I saying Blessing, and honour, and glory, and power, be unto him that sitteth upon the throne, and unto the Lamb for ever and ever. And the four beasts said, Amen. And the four and twenty elders fell down and worshipped Him that liveth for ever and ever"*(Revelation 5: 12-14).

What a day that will be!

We will be present because our faith is in the Lord Jesus Christ, who is:

- Head over all things (Ephesians 1:22).
- Firstborn from the dead (Colossians 1:18).
- Lamb of God (John 1:36).
- Lord of glory (1 Corinthians 2:8).
- Our Redeemer (Isaiah 43:4).
- Our Coming King (Revelation 1:7).

Where is Jesus now? He sits at the right hand of God (Mark 16:19), ready to make intercession for you to the Father.

By faith, you can ask the Risen Savior to forgive your sin, cleanse your heart and prepare a home in heaven for you.

CHAPTER 7

THE GOD OF MIRACLES

If you want to know if faith really works, don't ask a skeptic, or the person who has never taken the time to discover the world of Bible believing. Find someone with a valid personal testimony.

In the previous chapters we have discussed *why* we need to have faith and *how* to live with hope, expectation and belief. Now I want you to see the results.

In my years of ministry I have witnessed first-hand what Jesus spoke of when He said in the last days there would be signs, wonders and miracles.

Healing and deliverance did not end with the ministry of the disciples and apostles of the first century church. These are still taking place—and increasing in number as we near the Second Coming of Christ.

Let me share these stories.

IN JESUS' NAME

I recall the day I was asked to pray for a friend's grandmother. She was in her late 80s and wanted prayer for her knees.

At the time, I did not know she had not walked without physical aid or support for the last 12 years. I prayed for her in the name of Jesus Christ and, with faith and belief, gently eased her out of her chair (Acts 3:1-9).

She walked immediately without any aid or support.

About the same time I was also asked to pray for a woman who had been suffering with Grand Mal seizures for the previous 24 years.

After seeking all types of medical help the family had concluded she would probably have to live with this condition for the rest of her life. We prayed the prayer of faith for her.

She said "something warm" went through her body from her head to her toes. The woman knew instantly she was healed (Mark 5:29).

Today she gladly testifies of the miracle working power of God to all who will listen.

TOTALLY FREE!

In our church we often conduct services where we

pray for those who need a healing touch from God.

One Sunday there was a gentleman about 55 or 60 years of age. After the Lord revealed to me he had cancer, the individual confirmed it was cancer of the prostate.

We laid hands on him and claimed healing. The next day he told me, "After four years of constant pain, I am totally free." The suffering associated with the cancer was gone—and he was able to engage in activities he had not done for years.

Praise God!

A FINANCIAL MIRACLE

The Lord not only performs physical healings, but financial miracles as well.

One of the businessmen in our church was on the verge of bankruptcy—half a million dollars in debt and no hope of recovery. I felt led of the Spirit to tell him, "God wants to rescue your business."

> I FELT LED OF THE SPIRIT TO TELL HIM, "GOD WANTS TO RESCUE YOUR BUSINESS."

At this point he was open to anything because all else had miserably failed.

Together we united our voices in prayer and within days he was receiving contracts over the fax machine.

In less than a year God multiplied his enterprise abundantly—and today his business dealings run in the millions of dollars.

"A Tingling Feeling"

I vividly remember going home to visit my mother on a recent Mother's Day. While there I was talking with my cousin, who had a major physical problem.

About 14 years earlier he had been tragically shot in the back. As a result, his L-3 vertebrae was destroyed resulting in continual back pain and a severe limp in his right leg. "Would you let me pray for you?" I asked.

> "WOULD YOU LET ME PRAY WITH YOU?" I ASKED.

He agreed and we prayed in the name of Jesus and spoke faith to his spinal cord and back.

Immediately, He told me "a tingling feeling" pulsated through his body. He also announced the pain he had experienced for the last 14 years was gone.

I spoke with him a week later and he was walking pain-free.

The Doctor's Report

I also had the privilege of praying for a cousin who

had been admitted into the emergency room due to extremely high blood pressure. Her doctor ordered her not to return to work until it subsided.

After prayer she immediately reported "something hot" had gone into her body where my hand had touched her back and she believed she was healed.

The following day she visited her doctor and was told, "Go ahead and return to work. Your blood pressure is normal."

Thanks be to God!

NON-STOP TESTIMONIES

When faith and belief are present, miracles multiply.

Recently, ministering in South Hill, Virginia, the anointing of the Spirit was especially strong and I felt compelled to ask those who needed a physical healing to come forward for prayer. Before the service concluded it seemed nearly *everyone* present was anxious to testify.

One man was delivered from severe arthritis pain. Another gentleman who had no neurological sensitivity on the entire left side of his body was healed. Next, a woman who had practically zero range of motion on her left rotator cup was healed and rejoicing!

Yet another testified he could not use his left hand due to a chain saw injury. After prayer, he demonstrated to the congregation how his fingers were now back to normal.

Not only did we witness miracles of healing, but of salvation. There was great joy in South Hill that night (Acts 8:8). The works of the Lord were manifest and God was glorified (John 9:1-6). He alone is worthy!

> **THERE WAS GREAT JOY IN SOUTH HILL THAT NIGHT. THE WORKS OF THE LORD WERE MANIFEST AND GOD WAS GLORIFIED.**

IT HAPPENED TO CHRISTIAN

Recently, I received this written testimony from a couple in our church. I believe the miracle they witnessed in the life of their son, Christian, will build your faith.

On the morning of Tuesday, March 8, my wife and I found our son (Christian) lying in his room complaining of severe head pain and an inability to move. Immediately we called 911 who dispatched the paramedics. When they arrived, we learned Christian had a fever of 105.8 F with a rapid heart rate. We began praying in the spirit and laying hands on our son.

As the week progressed, Christian continued

86

to suffer from a high fever with chills. He slowly lost his appetite and became severely lethargic. He also began to complain of leg pain. We took Christian to his pediatrician, intermittently, to monitor his status.

In addition, we contacted our pastor who prayed with us about Christian's health. He prayed specifically that his heart, and other organs function normally. At the time, we had no idea this was a prophetic prayer.

On Thursday, March 10, Christian continued to have a high fever and did not appear to display any signs of improvement. Out of frustration, we took him to the hospital. The ER physician said he was suffering from a virus that was "going around" and that he would improve.

Christian's condition worsened throughout the course of the day and he refused to walk independently. He slept practically all day and could not hold eating utensils or sit up without assistance.

By late Friday night, our son could not walk, open his mouth, hold his head up or raise his arms. At this point, I honestly think my wife and I were focused on what we were seeing. Fear began to sink into both of us and we were overwhelmed by the site of our son deteriorating before our eyes.

On Saturday, March 12, Christian was admitted to the hospital. His condition was such that he was rushed to the Pediatric Intensive Care Unit (PICU). He was initially diagnosed with Guillian-Buerres syndrome until his body began to display multi-organ involvement.

His resting heart rate was 170 beats per minute (BPM), (he also had a disease called KAWASAKI which made his heart race. It can cause heart attacks in kids), his urine was red because we learned his body was destroying muscle tissue and passing it through the kidney.

In addition, the myeline sheath (covers and protects nerves) was also being destroyed. His liver was inflamed and his liver function tests (LFTs) were severely elevated. His platelet level was 20K (normal range is 150 - 250K) which basically meant he was at a high risk of internal bleeding with no clotting ability in his blood.

Even more, the high fever continued to persist. Physicians (neurologists, pediatricians, attendants, etc.) were baffled by Christian's clinical presentation.

His prognosis was gloom and we were told to prepare for him to be in the PICU a minimum of one month before we would see 'slight' improvement in his condition. We were also told that our son would get worse before/if he improved.

At that moment my wife and I knew that we needed to STRONGLY invoke our dominion & authority as children of God on our son's health. We began to pool together scriptures about health and healing and exercising our faith.

In addition, the Lord recalled to my wife the specifics of the prayer our pastor prayed. We began to refute everything the doctors told us. For example, when they said, "Your son will be sick for a while and will not walk for a year," we countered with, "We believe he is healed and will walk out of this hospital shortly."

We lived and breathed the Word and kept a Bible with us at all times. We both studied non-stop and began to ask the Lord to help us proclaim that we believe He has already healed Christian. We (separately) asked the Lord to remove fear from both of us.

Instead of allowing people to pray for Christian's healing, we asked them to agree and speak what we ALREADY believed had been DONE.

As we began to grow in faith, we would speak specifically to parts in Christian's body. My wife began to speak to his kidney and bladder and spoke against the protein in his urine. By Tuesday, March 15, his urine was clear. We spoke to his fever and it was gone by Thursday, March 17.

I spoke specifically to his heart rate—and endured a spiritual battle on Tuesday, March 15. By the next morning his heart rate was normal.

We both began speaking to his arms, legs, and throat muscles. On Friday, March 18, our son was able to stand on his feet. He regained the ability to use his arms and hands. He was able to use his mouth and swallow. His personality returned.

Physicians were astounded at the rapid progress he had made.

We learned that there is a reality and then there is the TRUTH. The TRUTH is what frees us. It does not matter what the circumstance, the Word of God is forever.

His Word teaches us He is the same today, yesterday and forevermore. We had to admit to our fear and ask God to remove it before we were able to stand on His Word. I believe His

Word and His Holy Spirit intervened and strengthened us.

We are here to say that faith and believing is not a fad. It works! Trust in the Lord in ALL things and lean not to your/man/the circumstance's understanding.

Thanks be to God, who reigns forever!

I rejoiced with these parents over the miracle which took place in Christian's life. It was only 16 days from the time of his illness until his complete recovery. Praise God!

> **IT WAS ONLY 16 DAYS FROM THE TIME OF HIS ILLNESS UNTIL HIS COMPLETE RECOVERY.**

THE HEALING POWER OF SCRIPTURE

Here are the specific scriptures these faith-filled parents used as they spoke the Word of God over their son:

- *"...by whose stripes* [Christian was] *healed"* (1 Peter 2:24).
- *"Yea, though I walk through the valley of the shadow of death, I will fear no evil"* (Psalm 23:4).

- I *"shall be able to quench all the fiery darts of the wicked"* (Ephesians 6:16).
- *"Resist the devil, and he will flee from you"* (James 4:7).
- *"Be not overcome of evil, but overcome evil with good"* (Romans 12:21).
- *"So shall my word be that goeth forth out of my mouth: it shall not return unto me void, but it shall accomplish that which I please, and it shall prosper in the thing whereto I sent it"* (Isaiah 55:11).
- *"And they overcame...by the blood of the Lamb, and by the word of their testimony"* (Revelation 12:11).
- *"Forever, O Lord, thy word is settled in heaven"* (Psalm 119:89).
- *"* [It is] *impossible for God to lie"* (Hebrews 6:18).
- *"*[Christian] *shall not die, but live, and declare the works of the Lord"* (Psalm 118:17).

IT'S STILL HAPPENING!

I am happy to report that God is still in the miracle-working business. If you read His Word, stand on His promises and believe, He will act on your behalf. As scripture declares, *"He that spared not His own Son, but delivered Him up for us all, how shall He not with*

Him also freely give us all things?" (Romans 8:32).

The reason the days of miracles are not over is because the God of Miracles is still alive and present! Jesus continues to say, *"If thou canst believe, all things are possible to him that believeth"* (Mark 9:23).

The Almighty is ready and able to perform signs, wonders and miracles, however, He works in conjunction with your believing. If you speak His Word from your mouth and believe with your heart, He will do more than you can ask or think!

CHAPTER 8

THE WORLD, THE FLESH, THE DEVIL

The New Testament is replete with information regarding the world and the "world system." Yet, there is still confusion and lack of knowledge as to what "the world" is—and how it relates to our faith as believers.

Many seem to think "living like the world" only refers to our style of dress and our musical preferences. It is much more indeed.

There are two Greek words found in the New Testament that refer to the world. One is where we derive the English word "cosmos"—referring to the planetary bodies and its inhabitants. The other is "eon" or "age" meaning a certain time frame in which a group of people live.

In Christ Jesus we have dominion over both of these—the physical world (Genesis 1:26-28) and the age in which we live (Romans 12:2).

According to scripture it is Satan who is the god of our planet. As Paul writes, *"In whom the god of this world hath blinded the minds of them which believe not, lest the light of the glorious gospel of Christ, who is the image of God, should shine unto them"* (2 Corinthians 4:4).

How did Satan attain this title and the power and authority which accompanies it? Adam gave it to him (Genesis 3:1-2; Luke 4:5-6)—since we know God would not have granted the devil such rule.

When the Father placed Adam in charge of His creation on earth, he became the "god of the world." However, when Adam disobeyed the Creator in the garden, he handed his God-given position and authority to the Evil One. Consequently, Satan became the new "god of the world."

THE FIRST "FAITH" MESSAGE

Prior to the fall of man, the world was where the first couple—and Adam's "order of things"—expressed and manifested themselves. This "Adamic" place was governed by faith in the Word of God, the angels and perpetual Holy Spirit involvement. There was no fear, only faith. In addition, there was no death or disease.

The first message preached by Satan in the garden to Adam was one of "faith"—the wrong kind with an evil objective. In a tragic mistake, Adam listens to the voice of his wife instead of the voice of God (Genesis 3:17) which is outright rebellion and spiritual betrayal.

Adam and Eve are now "born again" to death. Instead of eternal life (the nature of God), they have the nature of their new father, Satan (Ephesians 2:1-3; John 8:42-44). The original act associated with their "new birth" is to eat of the Tree of the Knowledge of Good and Evil.

> ADAM AND EVE ARE NOW "BORN AGAIN" TO DEATH. INSTEAD OF ETERNAL LIFE, THEY HAVE THE NATURE OF THEIR NEW FATHER, SATAN.

Disobeying God and tasting the forbidden fruit (an act of unrighteousness) is their first corresponding action associated with believing in the word of Satan. It is their initial "act of faith" related to their union with the devil.

HE HID HIMSELF

Prior to their rebellion, Adam and his wife lived and walked in light, love and faith. They also had the Holy Spirit and a multitude of angels who helped in every detail of their existence.

This was the place where the first two human creatures expressed themselves and their union with the Father. When this all changed, the world became Satan's place of expression.

Now, with the devil as the god of the world, Adam's first report to the Almighty is, *"I was afraid, because I was naked; and I hid myself"* (Genesis 3:10).

Fear is the "faith" of the devil, and Satan-filled circumstances now rule Adam's life. Where once there was righteousness and life, there is now death and unrighteousness. Satan is Adam's new father and the world is Adam's enemy.

MAN'S NEW RELATIONSHIP

Everything about the world has become "anti-Adam" and the curse was now earth's power and driving force (Genesis 3:17-19, Galatians 3:13).

Life was dethroned and death reigned (Romans 5:12-14). As scripture describes it, *"...the whole world lieth in wickedness"* (1 John 5:19).

Man's destruction is interwoven in the fabric of Adam's relationship with the world. He can no longer trust it, nor be sustained by it, without working by the sweat of his brow (Genesis 3:18-19).

The place created by the Father for Adam to flourish and thrive is now an instrument of Satan. It overcomes Adam at every turn—and also builds a barrier which keeps out the Father, the Holy Spirit and the angels of God. Where once the earth supported righteousness and faith, it has become a cistern of unholiness, sickness and disease.

The world's course is now a path of destruction and death fueled by its master, Satan (Ephesians 2:2; Hebrews 2:14-15; 2 Corinthians 4:4).

WORDS OF FEAR

Before the fall, the world supported man's belief and trust in God. The powers of heaven moved in tandem with Adam in all he did, and *together* they created (Genesis 2:19-20).

Laws of faith, believing, love and righteousness prevailed and permeated everything. Now, with Satan as the new god of the world, fallen angels (Luke 10:17-19) and demons (Ephesians 6:12) worked with Adam's *fear*-

> **THE RULE OF HATE, UNRIGHTEOUSNESS, FEAR AND UNBELIEF TOWARD GOD NOW CONTROLLED THE COURSE OF EVENTS.**

filled words perpetuating death and destruction.

As Job would later say: *"For the thing which I greatly feared is come upon me, and that which I was afraid of is come unto me"* (Job 3:25).

The rule of hate, unrighteousness, fear and unbelief toward God now controlled the course of events (Psalm 82:5; Ephesians 2:2).

A Puppet to Unseen Forces

Prior to the serpent making his appearance, Adam, with the angels, cooperated to promote the will of the Father in all things. With Satan and *his* angels now in charge, unwitting man was influenced to grow independent of God's Word and His law.

Instead of being a master, man was now a puppet to the unseen forces and rulers of the world. It was true then and remains true to this day: *"...we wrestle not against flesh and blood, but against principalities, against powers, against the rulers of the darkness of this world, against spiritual wickedness in high places"* (Ephesians 6:12).

> **Instead of being a master, man was now a puppet to the unseen forces and rulers of the world.**

Cain, Adam's son, was influenced by the devil and spirits of selfishness, hate and murder to kill his own brother (Genesis 4:5-11, 1 John 4:11-15).

We also see the devil at work later in the Old Testament. Daniel talks of the prince of Persia fighting against an angel who brings Daniel understanding regarding the last days (Daniel 10:13). The prince of Persia, of course, is a ruler over a certain region spiritually and geographically assigned by Satan. He was overcome by Michael "the prince who protects" who assisted Daniel.

POWER OVER THE ENEMY

Jesus gives us a preview of Satan and the world's eternal defeat as He declares, *"Now is the judgment of this world: now shall the prince of this world be cast out"* (John 12:31).

Satan's influence over man was spoken of by Paul: *"And the servant of the Lord must not strive; but be gentle unto all men, apt to teach, patient, in meekness instructing those that oppose themselves; if God peradventure will give them repentance to the acknowledging of the truth; and that they may recover themselves out of the snare of the devil, who are taken captive by him at his will"* (2 Timothy 2:24-26).

Even though the devil is the prince and power of the air, as we read the New Testament, we see how believing on Christ gives us authority over the enemy. Paul speaks of *"the princes of this world"* (1 Corinthians 2:6-8) referring to the dethroned principalities and powers which would subdue us. These unseen, evil forces (Colossians 2:15) were defeated by our Lord Jesus Christ through His death, burial, resurrection from the dead and blood offering in the Holy of Holies (Hebrews 10:19).

We now reign over these powers in Christ (Ephesians 1:18-23).

A REPEATING CYCLE

The world is hostile toward man because it is fused with the devil and remains his chief place of expression.

Believers need to realize the power Satan exercises through circumstances to control people who walk by sight and not by their faith in the Word of God.

If Satan is the god of this world, it is logical to conclude the earth is the carrier of the devil's voice. He communicates fear through situations he arranges and evil reports he brings. These induce apprehension—resulting in more satanic involvement and failure. The cycle repeats itself until faith in the Word of God removes the fear (I John 4:18, I John 5:4-5).

Listen to the words of Jesus: *"My sheep hear my voice, and I know them, and they follow me"* (John 10:27). The voice of Jesus is the Word of God (John 12:49-50).

THE EVIL REPORT

Satan also has a voice.

Remember, the first evil report in scripture is when Adam tells God how he was fearful, without clothing and hid himself.

This is what happens when we are not aware of the

presence, provision and ability of the Father in our lives. Attempting to exist independent of scripture will always result in an absence God's supply.

The Creator asks Adam this question: *"Who told thee that thou wast naked? Hast thou eaten of the tree, whereof I commanded thee that thou shouldest not eat?"* (Genesis 3:11).

It was the *circumstance* (listening to the wrong voice) that told Adam he was naked. But now their circumstance has become Satan's voice. It communicates to Adam his shame and lack of provision.

Consequently, Adam brings back an evil report. He speaks to the Father what the world (which is now under Satan's influence) has spoken to him —perpetrating even more circumstances. The result is confusion and fear (the devil's version of faith).

THE DEVIL'S FAULT?

Circumstances are Satan's version of Holy Spirit manifestations. Between the folds and layers of all Satan-induced situations you will hear the voice of the Evil One.

CIRCUMSTANCES ARE SATAN'S VERSION OF HOLY SPIRIT MANIFESTATIONS.

I have observed when believers are first born again, they—and even many who have been saved for years—speak boldly about what the devil has said to them:

- "The devil told me I won't make it!"
- "The devil said my marriage will fail."
- "The devil said I was going to die."

It is amazing to me how easily people can hear the voice of Satan, yet they have to pray and pray all night to hear what God is saying to them!

Since Satan speaks through circumstances, you don't even need to be spiritual to hear what he says. Here's how it works:

- Circumstances is the voice.
- A Satan-influenced world is the carrier.
- Fear is the spark which sets it all in motion.

We are familiar with the troubles of Job, but look at his statement of fear: *"For the thing which I greatly feared is come upon me, and that which I was afraid of is come unto me"* (Job 3:25).

Job's circumstances were the children of his fears, and the incessant evil reports began to follow. Satan's expressions to the world regarding Job was murder, destruction, stealing and a great wind (Job 1:14-19).

These ignited even more fear.

WHY BAD THINGS KEEP HAPPENING

Jesus told the religious leaders of His day, *"...ye seek to kill me, because my word hath no place in you"* (John 8:37). He explained, *"I speak that which I have seen with my father, and ye do that which ye have seen with your father* [Satan]" (John 8:38).

He also told them they could not understand His speech because they could not hear His word (John 8:43). Why? Because *"He that is of God heareth God's words: ye therefore hear them not, because ye are not of God"* (John 8:47).

When we fail to listen to the Word of God, in all likelihood we are attuned to the god of this world as he speaks through the events of our lives. Soon, fear and apprehension cause us to "tune in" to the devil's wavelength and our eyes are suddenly focused on our problems. As a result our speech is nothing more than an evil report—Satan's language.

> **WHEN WE FAIL TO LISTEN TO THE WORD OF GOD, IN ALL LIKELIHOOD WE ARE ATTUNED TO THE GOD OF THIS WORLD AS HE SPEAKS THROUGH THE EVENTS OF OUR LIVES.**

Being trapped in this cycle, we unwittingly continue the world's dominance in our lives. Is it any wonder bad things keep happening to us?

VOICES OF FEAR

Once, Jesus was ministering near the Sea of Galilee when one of the synagogue rulers, named Jairus, fell at His feet and pleaded earnestly, *"My little daughter lieth at the point of death: I pray thee, come and lay thy hands on her, that she may be healed; and she shall live"* (Mark 5:23).

In this arena of faith, the devil planted his evil report. The Bible says, *"there came from the ruler of the synagogue's house certain which said, thy daughter is dead: why troublest thou the master any further?"* (Mark 5:35).

This is the voice of "the god of this world, " using the situation to induce fear. Without, question Satan would have destroyed this man's daughter.

THE LORD TOTALLY IGNORED BOTH THE CIRCUMSTANCES AND THE EVIL REPORT.

What does the Master do? *"As soon as Jesus heard the word that was spoken, he saith unto the ruler of the synagogue, Be not afraid, only believe"*(Mark 5:36).

Notice, the Lord totally ignored both the circumstances and the evil report. He simply asked the man to believe the Word of God regarding his daughter, not the voice of this world.

Then, when Jesus arrived at the man's home, He

106

heard more of the same pessimism. There was a loud commotion, with people crying and wailing.

The Great Physician walked in and said, *"Why make ye this ado, and weep? the damsel is not dead, but sleepeth"* (v.38).

The Bible records He asked all of these nay-sayers to leave the house. Then He took the child's father, mother, and the disciples who were with Him, and went into the girl's room. There, he held her by the hand and said, *"Damsel, I say unto thee, arise"*(Mark 5:41).

This was the only voice that mattered. Immediately, the girl who had been given up for dead, stood to her feet and began to walk!

THE TRUE VOICE

The next time the Father of Lies attempts to fill your thoughts with gloom and doom, turn the tables on him. Let him know you are listening to the true voice —the voice of the Lord. Jesus says, *"These things I have spoken unto you, that in me ye might have peace. In the world ye shall have tribulation: but be of good cheer; I have overcome the world"* (John 16:33).

If you trust in the Father you no longer need to fear negative reports. In the words of the psalmist, *"He shall not be afraid of evil tidings: his heart is fixed, trusting in the Lord. His heart is established, he shall not be afraid"* (Psalm 112:7-8).

DIVINE DECLARATIONS

To Joshua and Caleb, it was immaterial what the world said. The bickering, complaining and negative attitude of the children of Israel were no match for what they saw in Canaan through the eyes of faith. As a result they spoke only the words of the Living God (Numbers 13:30-33;14:6-24).

Today, if you are ready to put Satan in his place and reclaim the dominion God has given you as His son or daughter, make these ten divine declarations yours:

1. *I will not love the world nor the things that are in the world* (1 John 2:15-17).
2. *God has not given me the spirit of fear, but of power and love and of a sound mind* (2 Timothy 1:7).
3. *I will live by every word that proceeds from the mouth of my Father* (Matthew 4:4).
4. *I will trust in the Lord and be of good courage, and He will strengthen my heart* (Psalm 31:24).
5. *No weapon formed against me shall prosper* (Isaiah 54:17).
6. *The Word of God will not depart out of my mouth, I will meditate on it night and day* (Joshua 1:8).

7. *I know that God will fill my life with good things* (Psalm 103:1-5).

8. *I will put on the whole armor of God so I will be able to stand against the wiles of Satan* (Ephesians 6:11).

9. *The Lord is my light and my salvation. I will not fear* (Psalm 27:1).

10. *I will not be conformed to this world, but be transformed by the renewing of my mind* (Romans 12:2).

Let Satan know he has no place in your life. Boldly claim what Jesus declared: *"Ye are of God, little children and have overcome them: because greater is He that is in you than He that is in the world. They are of the world, and the world heareth them. We are of God: he that knoweth God heareth us; and he that is not of God heareth not us. Hereby know we the spirit of truth, and the spirit of error"* (John 4:4-6).

The world is under your feet—Satan has been judged, dethroned and made powerless. Don't allow him to tell your otherwise!

Stand firm!

CHAPTER 9

LOOSING HEAVEN

By faith and belief you have been given the keys to the Kingdom of heaven.

With this trust comes a tremendous responsibility—especially regarding what we do as believers while we are still living on earth. This duty and obligation is what I describe as "loosing heaven."

Let me explain.

Speaking to Peter and the disciples, Jesus reveals insightful details concerning His plans for His church—including these words: *"...upon this rock* [revelation] *I will build my church; and the gates of hell shall not prevail against it"* (Matthew 16:18).

The revelation was the fact that Jesus is the Christ.

NO LONGER STRANGERS

The Son of God came and preached peace to those who were *"afar off"* [Gentiles] and those who *"were nigh"* [Jews] (Ephesians 2:17).

Both Jew and Gentile are now, through the cross of Christ, *"no more strangers and foreigners, but fellow citizens with the saints, and of the household of God"* (Ephesians 2:19).

The two groups are united—one—and *"are built upon the foundation of apostles and prophets, Jesus Christ himself being the chief corner stone"* (Ephesians 2:20).

Jesus accomplished His mission. This is why He told Peter He would build His church on the revelation that He is the Christ. As you read Ephesians, Colossians and Philippians, you will find the accomplished work.

TOTAL ACCESS

IF I HAVE BEEN GIVEN THE KEYS TO GOD'S KINGDOM OF HEAVEN, I ALSO KNOW HE WANTS ME TO SHARE WHAT IS INSIDE.

The believer is the church, and, according to Matthew 16:19, we have been given the keys to the Kingdom of heaven.

What are we to do with them?

Since a key is designed to open what is locked, we have been given access to something which would otherwise be closed. So, if I have been given the keys to God's Kingdom of heaven, I also know He wants me to share what is inside.

As a result of this trust, nothing related to heaven

should be denied me. Jesus says it is given to the redeemed *"to know the mysteries of the kingdom of heaven"* (Matthew 13:11).

Also, through Christ, we *"have access by one Spirit unto the Father"* (Ephesians 2:18). Plus, *"we have boldness and access with confidence by the faith of Him* [Jesus Christ]*"* (Ephesians 3:12).

YOUR AUTHORITY

The writer of Hebrews reminds us of this same truth: *"Having therefore, brethren, boldness to enter into the holiest by the blood of Jesus, ...let us draw near with a true heart in full assurance of faith, having our hearts sprinkled from an evil conscience, and our bodies washed with pure water"* (Hebrews 10:19, 22).

We find additional encouragement in these words: *"Let us therefore come boldly unto the throne of grace, that we may obtain mercy and find grace to help in time of need"* (Hebrews 4:16). And we are told, *"Fear not, little flock; for it is your Father's good pleasure to give you the kingdom"* (Luke 12:32).

From these verses I can stand on the assurance of the Word that I have unlimited and uninhibited access to the Kingdom of heaven.

The keys have also given me *authority* in both the Kingdom above and here on earth (Philippians 2:5-9; Romans 5:17).

113

BINDING AND LOOSING

Not only have we been entrusted with the keys, we have been placed in charge of a decision-making, authoritative role. Jesus says, *"...and whatsoever thou shalt bind on earth shall be bound in heaven: and whatsoever thou shalt loose on earth shall be loosed in heaven"* (Matthew 16:19).

Viewed another way, if a follower of Christ is binding on earth, it is being bound in heaven—and if the believer is loosing on earth, it is being loosed in heaven.

The moment you become a Christian, you are now heaven's representative. We are *"ambassadors for Christ"* (2 Corinthians 5:20).

THE DISTRIBUTION POINT

As I often say, we are "heaven's loading dock." Any goods from heaven to earth come via the body of Christ. As James writes, *"Every good gift and every perfect gift is from above, and cometh down from the Father of lights"* (James 1:17).

Whatever the Father accomplishes on earth, He does through His sons and daughters—we are heaven's distribution point.

Another way of looking at this is the analogy of a bank. We know each has a headquarters with many branches which are authorized to conduct business in the name of that particular bank. Well, heaven is God's headquarters and we, the followers of Christ, are the branch offices. We have been authorized to operate in the name of heaven. As Jesus says, *"I am the vine, ye are the branches"* (John 15:5).

> **WE HAVE BEEN AUTHORIZED TO OPERATE IN THE NAME OF HEAVEN.**

It's all part of our commission to "loose heaven" on earth.

DOING HIS WILL

In what we now call the "Lord's Prayer," Jesus asks the disciples to pray, *"...thy will be done in earth, as it is done in heaven"* (Matthew 6:10).

These words reinforce what the Father wants to accomplish. The disciples were commanded to manifest or "loose" whatever the will of the Father is in heaven into the earth—and this has dynamic implications.

1. Since there is no sickness in heaven, they were to loose heaven's healing into the earth
(2 Chronicles 7:14; Matthew 8:17; Luke 13:11-16; Acts 9:32-43; Acts 10:38; James 5:14-16).

2. Since there is no poverty in heaven, they were to loose heaven's wealth into the earth
(Deuteronomy 8:18; Malachi 3:10-12; Matthew

6:19-21; Luke 6:38; 2 Corinthians 9:1-15;
Philippians 4:17-19; 3 John 1:2).

3. **Since there is no fear in heaven, they were to
   loose heaven's faith into the earth** (Romans
   10:17; 1 Corinthians 1:17-31; 2 Timothy 1:7).

These are just three of an endless list of benefits
of "loosing" heaven.

YOUR QUALIFICATIONS

You may feel inadequate and think, "I'm not
qualified to release anything of a heavenly nature into
the earth."

I beg to differ. The Father has made us eminently
qualified to manifest all of His will into the world. He
*"hath made us meet to be partakers of the inheritance
of the saints in light"* (Colossians 1:12).

Remember, we are to be *"doers of the Word and
not hearers only"* (James 1:22).

Here is your new resumé:

- *You are a son of God* (1 John 3:1).
- *You are a vessel containing heavenly treasure*
  (2 Corinthians 4:7).
- *You are a new creation in Christ*
  (2. Corinthians 5:17).

- ***Your body is the temple of the Holy Ghost***
  (Romans 8:11; 2 Corinthians 6:14-18;
  1 Corinthians 6:19-20).
- ***God has enabled and placed you in
  ministry*** (1Timothy 1:12).
- ***God has established and anointed you***
  (2 Corinthians 1:21).
- ***You are washed, sanctified and justified in the
  name of the Lord Jesus*** (1 Corinthians 6:11).
- ***God works in you both to will and to do His
  good pleasure*** (Philippians 2:13).
- ***You are the workmanship of God and were
  created in Christ Jesus unto good works***
  (Ephesians 2:10).

The Bible is literally filled with scriptures which remind us of what the Father has done for you and me—revealing how truly qualified we are to loose heaven.

RELEASING RESOURCES

What are the assets of heaven we are to release on earth? Here are just a few:

1. ***Angels*** (Psalm 103:20).
2. ***The gifts of the Spirit*** (1 Corinthians.12:7-10).
3. ***The Love of God*** (Romans 5:5).

117

4. The peace of God (John 14:27; Philippians 4:6-7).
5. The strength of God (Colossians 1:11;
    Ephesians 3:16; Psalm 71:16; Psalm 84:5-7).
6. The joy of the Lord (Nehemiah 8:10; John
    15:11).
7. The Wisdom of God (1 Corinthians 1:30;
    James 1:5; James 3:13-17).

—plus many more heavenly treasures we are to set free in the earth (John 3:12, Colossians 3:1-4).

RESTORING THE BRIDGE

As you study God's Word, you will find practically everything a believer does opens a door of involvement for the Father and His resources. God passionately desires to be engaged and participating in the affairs of earth, yet He has pledged to work through His people: *"For it is God which worketh in you both to will and to do of his good pleasure"* (Philippians 2:13).

> PRACTICALLY EVERYTHING A BELIEVER DOES OPENS A DOOR OF INVOLVEMENT FOR THE FATHER AND HIS RESOURCES.

We also know, *"The heaven, even the heavens, are the Lord's: but the earth hath he given to the children of men"* (Psalm 115:16).

When man disobeyed in the garden, a two-fold

118

tragedy occurred:

1. The unbelief unleashed into the earth through Satan's deception denies man access to the Father and all of Heaven's resources.
2. This same unbelief denies the Father access to earth.

The keys of heaven being given to the church resolves this problem. By presenting these keys, the child of God has been given access and authority into the heavenly Kingdom—and the Kingdom has been given access and authority into the earth.

The bridge has been restored; the two have become one (John 17:10,20-23).

THE ACTIVATION

You can own a collection of a thousand keys, but what are their value unless you place one in the opening of a lock and a door opens?

The Name of Jesus represents such a key because it has been given to the believer to be used authoritatively on earth (Acts 4:12; Philippians 2:5-12). There is no name above the precious name of Jesus. We have been given this great and mighty weapon which literally makes the devil flee (James 4:7) and allows us to move offensively—and with dominion—throughout the Earth.

Everything the child of God does representing heaven becomes a key. Let me share a few examples.

- The Word tells me to ask and I will receive (John 16:24). Receive from Whom? Heaven.
- The Word tells me to seek and I shall find (Matthew 7:7). Who reveals what I seek? Heaven.
- The Word tells me to knock and it shall be opened. Who does the opening? Again, heaven (Acts 14:27, Revelation 3:7-8).
- The Word tells me to turn from my wicked ways, humble myself and pray and I will hear from where? Heaven. (2 Chronicles 7:14).
- The Word tells me to tithe (Malachi 3:10-12) and God will open the windows of Heaven and pour out a blessing that there shall not be room enough to receive it.
- The Word tells me to give and it shall be given to me; good measure, pressed down, shaken together and running over (Luke 6:38). Men may do the giving, yet heaven is behind the act.
- The Word tells me if I can believe, all things are possible (Mark 9:23). Heaven's

involvement makes it a reality.
- The Word tells me that my sowing causes
  God (Heaven) to make all grace abound
  toward me (the believer) so I will have
  sufficiency in all things and abound to every
  good work (2 Corinthians 9:6-8).
- The Word tells me to lay up for myself
  treasures in Heaven where neither moth nor
  rust corrupts and where thieves do not break
  through and steal (Matthew 6:19-21).

Every time a member of the body of Christ obeys the Word of God and *believes* in what he is doing, he is opening earth to heaven and heaven to earth.

The Holy Spirit is involved with our acts of faith. So whenever I am using the name of Jesus, whether I am giving, sowing, tithing, praying, confessing, binding or loosing I am invoking heaven's involvement in the earth. I am releasing heaven!

AS HE IS, SO ARE WE

Before I became a born again Christian, every action of my life was devoid of heaven's involvement. Now, because I am built upon the foundation of the apostles and prophets—with Jesus Christ being the chief cornerstone—heaven is the *reason* for my activities. The Father has *"raised us up together, and made us sit together in heavenly places in Christ Jesus"* (Ephesians 2:6).

From this position of power, the believer binds and looses by his obedience to the Word of God. Never forget that what is being either released or bound is ours to do. Scripture tell us, *"as he* [Jesus] *is, so are we in this world"* (1 John 4:17).

Don't accept the keys to the Kingdom and treat them casually. Operate from a position of faith and believing to distribute heavenly goods to the millions who are waiting to experience an outpouring from above.

CHAPTER 10

THE DYNAMICS OF EFFECTUAL PRAYER

The most significant foundation stone in the life of any born again Christian is prayer. It is the firm and secure base on which a house of faith and a structure of belief is built.

Prayer is also multi-faceted: it is a tool, a weapon, a door, a guide and a roadmap. It gives us dynamic access to the unlimited resources of heaven and the Kingdom of God.

In biblical Christianity there is no such thing as life in Christ without prayer. Why? Because a *prayerless* believer is a weak, *powerless* believer.

I also feel unanswered prayer should be an *abnormality*—the exception rather than the norm.

If Jesus went to such great lengths to secure our access and fellowship with God, how can we do less than spend time in His presence in praise in worship, adoration and prayer?

Later in this chapter we will discuss the characteristics of prayer, but first I want you to understand *why* we pray. Here are 20 valid reasons:

1. Prayer accomplishes God's work.

Just after Jesus said, *"the works that I do shall he do also; and greater works than these shall he do; because I go unto my Father"* (John 14:12), He told us how that would be possible: *"And whatsoever ye shall ask in my name, that will I do"* (John 14:13). Prayer helps complete the work of the Father.

2. Prayer helps determine God's will.

The Bible tells us not to be unwise, but *"understanding what the will of the Lord is"* (Ephesians 5:17). This is only possible through calling on God. Jesus teaches us to pray, *"Thy will be done"* (Matthew 6:10).

This is the key to walking lock-step with God.

3. Prayer provides fellowship with the Father.

Jesus says, *"Behold, I stand at the door, and knock: if any man hear my voice, and open the door, I will come in to him, and will sup with him, and he with me"* (Revelation 3:20).

Make certain the Lord is your closest friend.

4. Prayer is a defense against temptation.

We are warned: *"Watch and pray, that ye enter not into temptation: the spirit indeed is willing, but the flesh is weak"* (Matthew 26:41).

Ask the Lord to surround and protect you.

5. Prayer is a command of God.

"Praying always with all prayer and supplication in the Spirit, and watching thereunto with all perseverance and supplication for all saints; (Ephesians 6:18).

───────────■───────────

IT'S NOT A SUGGESTION, BUT AN ORDER!

It's not a suggestion, but an order!

6. Prayer is necessary for spiritual growth and maturity.

"And this I pray, that your love may abound yet more and more in knowledge and in all judgment" (Philippians 1:9).

You are much taller when you are on your knees!

7. Prayer invites the Lord to demonstrate His love.

David writes, *"I have called upon thee, for thou wilt hear me, O God: incline thine ear unto me, and hear my speech* [and] *show thy marvelous lovingkindness"* (Psalm 17:6-7).

The Lord listens and loves!

8. Prayer brings healing.

When prayer is combined with faith, all things are possible. *"And the prayer of faith shall save the sick, and the Lord shall raise him up"*(James 5:15).

Are you praying with total faith?

9. Prayer helps us influence the lives of others.

Paul wrote these words to Timothy: *"I exhort therefore, that, first of all, supplications, prayers, intercessions, and giving of thanks, be made for all men; For kings, and for all that are in authority; that we may lead a quiet and peaceable life in all godliness and honesty"* (1 Timothy 2:1-2).

Be certain your words are not always self-centered.

10. Prayer helps us follow Christ's example.

In each of the Gospels we find accounts of Jesus spending time in prayer. In Galilee, *"in the morning, rising up a great while before day, he went out, and departed into a solitary place, and there prayed"* (Mark 1:35). After healing a man with leprosy, Jesus, *"withdrew himself into the wilderness, and prayed"* (Luke 5:16).

If the Son of God needed to pray, how much more do we?

11. Prayer helps us focus on godly priorities.

We are counseled to *"give yourselves to fasting and prayer...that Satan tempt you not for your incontinency"* (1 Corinthians 7:5). *"But the end of all things is at hand: be ye therefore sober, and watch unto prayer"* (1 Peter 4:7).

What's important to God must also be vital to you.

■

WHAT'S IMPORTANT TO GOD MUST ALSO BE VITAL TO YOU.

---

12. Prayer is a means through which we confess our sin.

Nehemiah prayed, *"Let thine ear now be attentive, and thine eyes open, that thou mayest hear the prayer of thy servant, which I pray before thee now, day and night... and confess the sins of the children of Israel, which we have sinned against thee: both I and my father's house have sinned"* (Nehemiah 1:6).

Bring every transgression to the Father.

13. Prayer gives us strength.

The apostle Paul writes: *"For this cause I bow my knees unto the Father of our Lord Jesus Christ, Of whom the whole family in heaven and earth is named, That he would grant you, according to the riches of his glory, to be strengthened with might by his Spirit in the inner man"* (Ephesians 3:14-16).

Communion with the Lord brings power.

14. Prayer helps us become one in Christ.

Those who gathered in the Upper Room to wait for the promise of the father, *"all continued with one accord in prayer and supplication"* (Acts 1:14).

Unity brings revival!

15. Prayer demonstrates our trust in the Lord.

"If my people, which are called by my name, shall humble themselves, and pray, and seek my face, and turn from their wicked ways; then will I hear from heaven, and will forgive their sin, and will heal their land" (2 Chronicles 7:14).

Where will *you* turn for help?

16. Prayer pleases God.

In the words of King Solomon, *"The sacrifice of the wicked is an abomination to the Lord: but the prayer of the upright is his delight"* (Proverbs 15:8).

Let the Lord smile on your life.

17. *Prayer replaces worry and fear.*

"For the eyes of the Lord are over the righteous, and his ears are open unto their prayers...and if ye suffer for righteousness' sake, happy are ye: and be not afraid of their terror, neither be troubled" (1 Peter 3:12,14).

Fear not!

18. *Prayer is answered by God.*

The psalmist writes, *"My soul, wait thou only upon God; for my expectation is from him"* (Psalm 62:5).

There is only one ultimate source for the solution.

19. *Prayer changes our attitude.*

Jesus tells us to, *"Love your enemies, bless them that curse you, do good to them that hate you, and pray for them which despitefully use you, and persecute you"* (Matthew 5:44).

It's time for a *super*-natural response.

20. *Prayer works!*

Thrown in jail for preaching the Gospel, *"...at midnight Paul and Silas prayed, and sang praises unto God: and the prisoners heard them. And suddenly there was a great earthquake, so that the foundations of the prison were shaken: and immediately all the doors were opened, and every ones bands were loosed.* (Acts 16:25-26).

Prayer produces freedom and liberty!

Six Vital Steps

You may ask, "Am I doing it right? How should I pray? What should be my attitude and approach to the Father?"

Let me share these six elements of effectual prayer:

One: Pray with Faith

Faith can and will work without prayer; however, *prayer* cannot and will not work without faith.

God is not impressed with those who, out of habit, repeat words they have memorized. It is not only prayer, but *believing* prayer which brings results. This is exactly what Jesus tells us: *"Verily I say unto you, If ye have faith, and doubt not, ye shall not only do this which is done to the fig tree, but also if ye shall say unto this mountain, Be thou removed, and be thou cast into the sea; it shall be done. And all things, whatsoever ye shall ask in prayer, believing, ye shall receive"* (Matthew 21:21-22).

How? *Believing!*

What springs from your heart—true belief—is the

hinge upon which the door of effectual prayer swings. Petitions dominated by fear and doubt or majoring on "need" will only result in frustration.

The belief and trust you establish as a result of knowing God's Word allows you to pray with belief. As James the disciple states: *"But let him ask in faith, nothing wavering. For he that wavereth is like a wave of the sea driven with the wind and tossed. For let not that man think that he shall receive any thing of the Lord"* (James 1:6-7).

TWO: PRAY WITH CONFIDENCE

When it comes to effectual prayer there can be no accommodations for doubt. Uncertainty is a faith killer—it will dilute any hope or expectation and neutralize your believing.

UNCERTAINTY IS A FAITH KILLER.

Again, the cure for doubt is to build your life on the declarations of God found in scripture. It is where we build our confidence and establish our *position* in prayer.

John explains it is our strong certainty and belief in the Lord which brings results: *" ...if we ask anything according to His will He heareth us; and, if we know that He hear us, whatsoever we ask, we know that we have the petitions that we desired of Him. Whosoever shall confess that Jesus is the Son of God, God dwelleth in him, and he in God* (1 John 4:14-15).

This means even *before* I pray, I can be assured God will answer because I have asked according to His Word (His Word is His will).

This unparalleled confidence is at the grassroots of all effectual prayer.

THREE: PRAY WITH BOLDNESS

When you understand the significance of being forgiven and set free through the blood of the cross, you will walk with unabashed authority. As King Solomon writes, *"...the righteous are as bold as a lion"* (Proverbs 28:1).

SPIRITUAL BOLDNESS IS NOT ARROGANCE OR A HAUGHTY ATTITUDE.

Spiritual boldness, however, is not arrogance or a haughty attitude. Rather, it means we live without shame.

The Bible tells us to *"come boldly unto the throne of grace, that we may obtain mercy, and find grace to help in time of need"* (Hebrews 4:16).

This same assurance allows us to have *" boldness to enter into the holiest by the blood of Jesus"* (Hebrews 10:19) How? By *"a new and living way, which he hath consecrated for us"* (v.20).

This is what gives us the ability to *"draw near with a true heart in full assurance of faith"* (v.22).

When the reference point for your belief is what God has said, your life will perpetuate this fearless, even *daring,* boldness. For the Almighty has promised, *"I will never leave thee nor forsake thee. So that we might boldly say, The Lord is my helper, and I will not fear what man shall do unto me"* (Hebrews 13:5-6).

This is spiritual boldness and authority at its finest.

FOUR: PRAY WITH THANKSGIVING

People who are effectual in their prayers are the most God-appreciating men and women you will meet—constantly on the *receiving* end of the Lord's provision.

This is true because such individuals understand God is the Rewarder of those who diligently seek Him. They know the source of their blessings.

They also realize it is not a matter of time, *but a matter of prayer* before receiving answers to the petitions they desire from the Lord.

If you are looking for a results-based recipe for coming before the Father, use the ingredients recommended by the apostle Paul: *"Be careful for nothing; but in every thing by prayer and supplication with thanksgiving let your requests be made known unto God. And the peace of God, which passeth all understanding, shall keep your hearts and minds through Christ Jesus"* (Philippians 4:6-7).

Most Christians can quote the verse, *"Pray without ceasing"* (1 Thessalonians 5:17). They should also memorize the words which follow: *"In every thing give thanks: for this is the will of God in Christ Jesus concerning you"* (1 Thessalonians 5:18).

It should be no surprise our thanksgiving is an integral part of effective prayer—especially since the end result is receiving from God. Yes there are communion and fellowship aspects of prayer, but those too should include our thankfulness.

Also, gratitude is your faith expressing this: a basic understanding that what God has promised, He is able also to perform.

Even *before* Jesus raised Lazarus from the dead, He lifted His eyes up to the Father and said, *"I thank thee that thou hast heard me"* (John 11:41).

This was the precedent to a marvelous miracle from God.

Since Jesus is our example, *"By him therefore let us offer the sacrifice of praise to God continually, that is, the fruit of our lips giving thanks to his name"* (Hebrews 13:15).

Our communion with the Father must *never* be devoid of thanksgiving. It is the cornerstone upon which effectual prayer firmly rests.

FIVE: PRAY WITH PERSEVERANCE

Many become lost on the road to receiving from God because they do not practice prayer as a continuing lifestyle.

It is not enough to say, "Oh, I have prayed." We most develop the *habit* of prayer.

We need to pray diligently, non-stop—before, during and after the answer. This is what Daniel did when he needed to spare his own life

WE MUST DEVELOP THE HABIT OF PRAYER.

by interpreting Nebuchadnezzar's dream. He asked his friends to join with him to *"desire mercies of the God of heaven concerning this secret"* (Daniel 2:18).

When the dream was revealed to Daniel in a night vision, the Bible says he *"blessed the God of heaven"* (Daniel 2:19). His praying never ceased.

Fellowship with the Lord should be a common occurrence and a vital life function—as natural as eating, sleeping and breathing.

The importance of perseverance in prayer can't be overstated. Jesus says, *"...men ought always to pray, and not to faint"* (Luke 18:1). A few verses later He gives the explanation why: *"...and shall not God avenge His own elect, which cry day and night unto Him, though He bear long with them? I tell you that he will avenge them speedily"* (v.7).

In the early church it was the "tenacious" prayers of believers which secured Peter's release from King Herod's evil intentions—not the politics of compromise. The Bible records, *"Peter therefore was kept in prison: but prayer was made without ceasing of the church unto God for him"* (Acts 12:5)

The message from the Lord is, "Don't quit!"

SIX: BE SPECIFIC

To fully appreciate the power of prayer it is paramount to **harness your believing and target your faith.** Many erroneously assume since God is all-knowing, all-powerful, and all loving He will answer any general prayer. Don't assume too much!

In the story of blind Bartimaeus, Jesus asked him a pointed question: *"...what wilt thou that I should do unto thee?* (Mark 10:51).

It was obvious the man was blind, yet the Lord was looking for him to speak to a specific need.

Bartimaeus didn't ask for alms, or even petition Jesus on behalf of his friends. Instead, he gave this focused reply: *"Lord, that I might receive my sight"* (Mark 10:51).

It's important to note the Son of God did not walk over to the blind man and simply say: "Be healed." Jesus wanted to *see* belief—and He found it.

Bartimaeus knew precisely what he wanted Jesus to do for him.

The Lord looked at the man and said, *"Go thy way; thy faith hath made thee whole. And immediately he received his sight, and followed Jesus"* (v.52).

The prayer requests found in the New Testament are always specific—not general in nature. Scripture tells us to *"be careful for nothing but in everything by prayer and supplication with thanksgiving let your* [specific] *requests be made known unto God"* (Philippians 4:6).

Remember, *"the effectual fervent prayer of a righteous man availeth much"* (James 5:16).

We have explored two important questions: (1) "Why should I pray?" and (2) "How should I pray?" However, there is one more: "When should I pray?"

The answer is "Right now!"

IT'S A PROMISE!

By exercising faith, you bring life to the promises of God.

You can have total confidence in what the Father tells you since *"God is not a man, that he should lie"* (Numbers 23:19). Everything about Him is truth and light—*"...and in him is no darkness at all"* (1 John 1:5).

If God says it will come to pass, *it will!*

For the Word to become a tangible reality in your everyday life, put these words into practice:

> GOD'S PROMISE MUST BECOME
> YOUR PROFESSION, SO THAT HIS POWER
> CAN MAKE IT (that particular promise)
> YOUR POSSESSION.

I want you to remember these four distinct parts of this statement:

1. HIS PROMISE

All of God's blessings begin with His promises!

Scripture tells us, *"And this is the confidence that we have in him, that, if we ask any thing according to his will, he heareth us: And if we know that he hear us, whatsoever we ask, we know that we have* [present tense, right now] *the petitions that we desired of Him"* (1 John 5:14-15).

Let me encourage you to read Luke 1:30-45; Romans 4:16-21; Hebrews 6:11-18; 1 John 2:25.

2. YOUR PROFESSION

We must continually confess what the Lord has said concerning our situation—no matter how fearful it may look or how bad we may feel. God's provision is not based upon our feelings nor the change in the weather. It is founded upon the integrity and infallibility of scripture.

Don't stop claiming His Word: *"Let us hold fast the profession of our faith without wavering; (for he is faithful that promised;)"* (Hebrews 10:23).

Study Deuteronomy 30:11-14; Joshua 1:5-8; Isaiah 55:8-12; Mark 11:22-24.

3. HIS POWER

The Holy Spirit is the Person behind any manifestation of God's Word. Remember, it is *"Not by might, nor by power, but by my spirit, saith the Lord of hosts"* (Zechariah 4:6).

If we forget this, we foolishly attempt to operate in our own strength—and will ultimately fail. God's Spirit has been sent to work *for* us, *with* us and *in* us!

Read Genesis 1:2; 1 Samuel 16:13; Luke 1:34-35; 1 Corinthians 2:4-5.

4. YOUR POSSESSION

By faith, everything in heaven can be yours on earth right now. Love, joy, peace, grace, strength, finances, and the Spirit's anointing. As a matter of truth, these things *are* yours—part of your inheritance as a child of God.

Be inspired by the words of Psalm 81:10-16; Matthew 17:20; Mark 11:22-24; 2 Peter 1:2-4; 1 John 5:14-15.

I want to thank you for allowing me to walk with you on your journey of faith. Will you let God's promise become your profession? Will you invite His power to make it your possession?

Faith works. It really does!

Pastor André Gorham praying for healing and deliverance during a crusade in Manila, Philippines.

FOR A COMPLETE LIST OF RESOURCES, OR TO
SCHEDULE THE AUTHOR FOR SPEAKING
ENGAGEMENTS, CONTACT:

ANDRÉ GORHAM
ANOINTED WORD MINISTRIES
PHONE: 919-598-1879
INTERNET: www.anointed.org
EMAIL: pastor@anointed.org

COMMUNITY FELLOWSHIP INTERNATIONAL CHURCH
1812 RIDDLE ROAD
DURHAM, NC 27713
PHONE: 919-598-8555